The BIG BOOK OF KNOWLEDGE

The BIG BOOK OF KNOWLEDGE

p

This is a Parragon Publishing book
This edition published in 2006

Parragon Publishing
Queen Street House
4 Queen Street
Bath BA1 1HE

Copyright © Parragon Books Ltd 1999

This edition put together by Starry Dog Books Ltd

ISBN 978-1-4075-2425-2
Printed in China

Contents

INTRODUCTION

FACTS ARE ALL around us. Sometimes it seems there are too many facts for our brains to absorb. This book helps your brains by making the facts interesting and easy to understand. The facts are presented in fact panels and data panels on specific subjects, so the facts are easy to find.

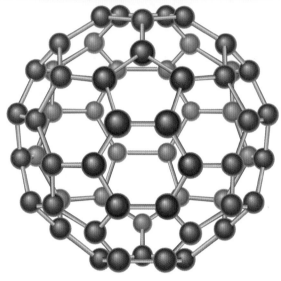

Fact Panels

Hundreds of key facts are provided in the fact panels. Each key fact has a bullet (·) to help you find it.

Captions also provide additional vital information.

Quizzes

At the end of each section is a quiz to test how well you remember the facts. Some of the answers are on the Key Facts pages, so don't forget to read these, too!

Categories

The book is also broken down into different categories, such as animals, science, plants, the Universe etc., to help you find the information you want quickly.

Superb illustrations throughout the book provide visual information to add to your fact-finding.

Amazing Fact finder

This is an atom. It is so tiny that two billion would fit on the dot on the top of this "i."

This is what a silicon chip looks like from 8 inches away. It is about 1/4 inch long.

This is what a butterfly looks like from about 3 feet away. It is about an inch across.

THIS BOOK CONTAINS a huge array of facts about everything from the smallest thing in the Universe to the biggest. The tiniest things in the Universe, such as atoms, are so small you can only see them under the most powerful microscopes. The very tiniest are particles called quarks, so small that billions of them would fit inside an atom. The biggest things, such as stars and galaxies, are so big you can only see them all when they are very far away. The very biggest is a wall of galaxies in space called the Great Wall, 800 million light-years long. In between come all kinds of things, from insects and the little electronic chips that make computers to large animals such as lions and us humans, and from great mountains and rivers to entire continents and the world.

This is what a lion looks like from about 30 feet away. It is about 10 feet long.

MEASUREMENTS

1,000 picometers	=	1 nanometer
1,000 nanometers	=	1 micrometer
1,000 micrometers	=	1 millimeter
10 mm	=	1 centimeter
100 cm	=	1 meter
1,000 m	=	1 kilometer
9,46 trillion km	=	1 light-year

SMALL THINGS & BIG THINGS

SMALL THINGS

• A Caesium atom is just 0.0000005 mm across.

• The smallest living thing is the bacteria *Mycoplasma laidlawii*, 0.1 micrometers long.

BIG THINGS

• The largest galaxy is at the center of the Abell 2029 galaxy cluster in the constellation of Virgo, thought to be 5.6 million light-years across.

• The largest structure made by living things is the coral Great Barrier Reef, off Queensland Australia, more than 1,200 miles long.

This is what our galaxy the Milky Way looks like from two million light-years away–that is, about 32 billion billion miles. It is about 100,000 light-years (about 600 billion miles) across.

This is what the Sun looks like from about 87 million miles away. It is about 800 million miles across.

This is what the Earth looks like from 60,000 miles away. The Earth is around 8,000 miles across.

This is what mountains such as the Matterhorn in the Alps look like from about 6 miles away. It is about 10,000 feet high.

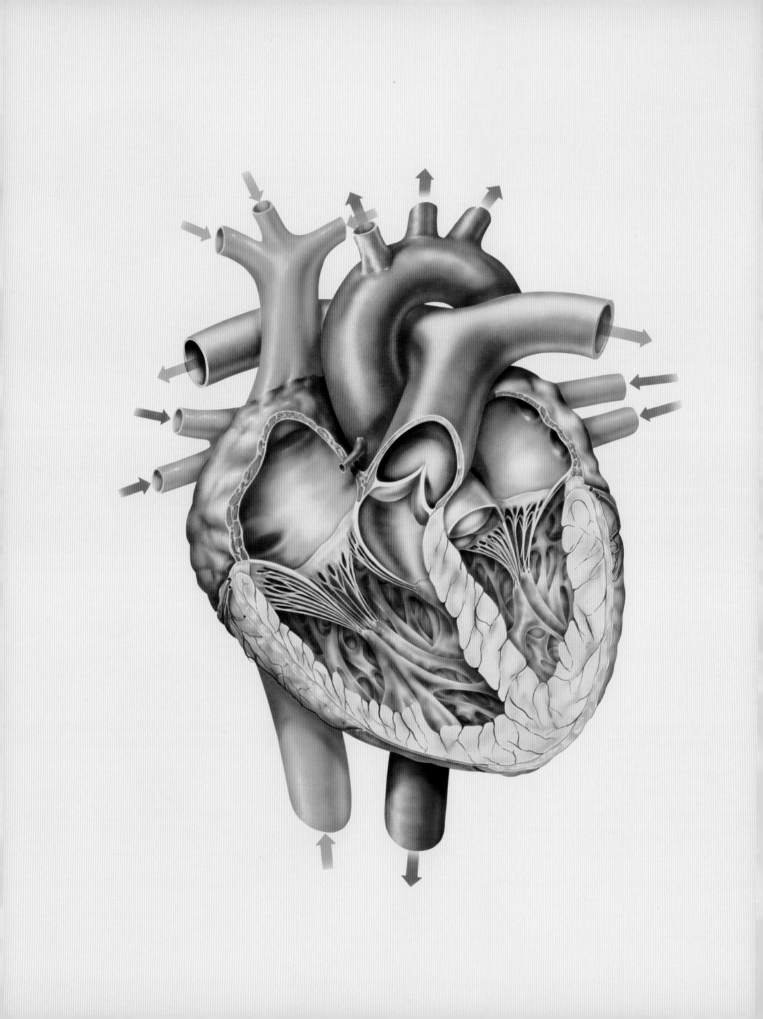

PEOPLE

Heart and blood

THE HEART IS ONE OF THE BODY'S MARVELS, pumping blood around the body ceaselessly. Every second of the day, even as you sleep, the heart's powerful muscles are contracting to send a jet of blood shooting through the body's intricate network of blood vessels. Blood flows right around the body and back to the heart, creating a complete circulation to every part of the body. Without it, you would quickly die. Blood carries the oxygen, nutrients, and chemicals that every body cell needs to survive, and washes away all the waste products, including carbon dioxide.

FACTS: About blood

- **What is blood?**
  It is a complex mix of cells and platelets in a clear yellowish fluid called plasma. Washed along in the plasma too are salts, hormones, fats, and sugars.

- **Red blood cells**
  The most numerous blood cells are button-shaped "red" blood cells, which are like rafts that ferry oxygen around the body, held on board by a protein called hemoglobin.

- **White blood cells**
  Big "white" blood cells play a vital role in the body's defense against disease. White blood cells called neutrophils swallow invaders. Lymphocytes help identify them.

- **Platelets**
  Tiny cell fragments called platelets help plug leaks, such as cuts.

▶ Blood is a mix of red cells (erythrocytes), white cells (leucocytes), and tiny platelets in plasma.

FACTS: About circulation

- **Arteries**
  Blood flows out from the heart through large blood vessels called arteries, which branch into smaller arterioles and then into tiny capillaries.

- **Veins**
  Blood flows back to the heart through small venules that join to form larger veins. The load of oxygen makes blood redder in the arteries than the veins.

- **Double circulation**
  There two systems of circulation in the body, each pumped by a different half of the heart.

- **Double circulation**
  The left of the heart drives the "systemic" circulation, which carries oxygen-rich blood from the lungs around the body. The right half of the heart drives the "pulmonary" circulation, which drives blood through the lungs to the left side of the heart.

- **Pulse**
  The pumping of the heart sends regular shock waves through the circulation, detectable as a pulse. To feel your pulse, lay two fingers gently on the inside of your wrist. Counting the number of pulses tells you how fast your heart is beating.

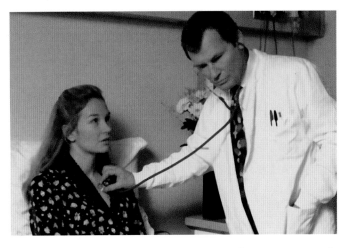

DATA: Blood & heart

- **RACING BLOOD**
  Blood flows through the arteries at 40 inches a second.

- **BLOOD VESSELS**
  There are 37,000 miles of capillaries in the body.

▲ *This doctor is checking his patient's risk of suffering from "coronary heart disease." In this disease, the supply of blood to the heart muscle is restricted in some way—and may be cut off altogether, causing a heart attack, in which the heart stops beating.*

Blood returning from the body floods from the vena cava into the right atrium

Blood from the left ventricle is pushed into the aorta

Blood goes off to the lungs via the pulmonary artery

Oxygenated blood returns from the lungs

Blood returning from the body gathers in the right atrium

Blood from the right ventricle is pushed into the pulmonary artery

Left atrium

Left ventricle

Valves ensure the blood flows only one way

▶ *The heart is not just one pump but two, separated by a thick wall of muscle called the septum. Blood from the veins flows into each half of the heart from the top, flooding the "atrium," the first of the two chambers. This is a small reservoir where blood builds up before entering the second chamber, or "ventricle." The ventricle has extra thick, muscular walls, which squeeze the blood out and send it shooting through the arteries.*

Septum separating the two halves

The body's biggest vein, the inferior vena cava

The body's widest artery, the aorta

13

Lungs

IF YOU STOPPED BREATHING, for more than a minute or two, you would quickly die. Breathing provides your blood with the oxygen from the air that is vital to the survival of every body cell. Just as fire burns only if there is plenty of oxygen, so body cells need oxygen from the blood to break down the food they also get from the blood. Without oxygen, brain cells live only a few minutes–which is why the brain is quickly damaged if the heart stops pumping blood. When cells break down food, oxygen joins with carbon in the food to make carbon dioxide, which you breathe out.

FACTS: About breathing

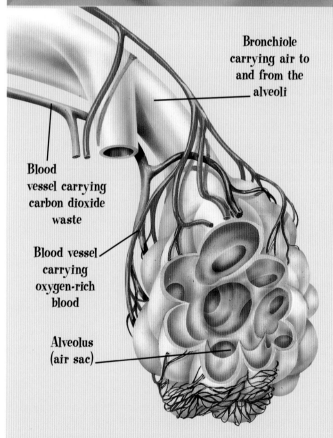

Bronchiole carrying air to and from the alveoli

Blood vessel carrying carbon dioxide waste

Blood vessel carrying oxygen-rich blood

Alveolus (air sac)

▲ At the end of every airway in the lung, there are clusters of tiny air sacs called alveoli–more than 300 million altogether. This is where oxygen is transferred into the blood. The "blue" blood vessels carry carbon dioxide to the alveoli ready for breathing out. The "red" vessels carry fresh oxygen to the rest of the body.

- **Nose and throat**
  Normally, you breathe air in through your nose—although you can also breathe through your mouth. Air then flows down through your throat through a tube—called the pharynx—at the top, the larynx in the middle, and the trachea at the bottom.

- **Two lungs**
  The trachea pipes air into your lungs, the two spongy grayish-pink bags in your chest. Lungs transfer oxygen from the air into the blood.

- **Airways**
  The lungs are like hollow trees with hundreds of branching airways called bronchioles.

- **Air sacs**
  Around the end of each bronchiole are clusters of air sacs, or "alveoli," like bunches of grapes.

- **Air to blood**
  When you breathe in, oxygen from the air passes through the thin walls of the alveoli into the tiny blood vessels wrapped around them.

- **Blood to air**
  Unwanted carbon dioxide passes from the blood through the alveoli walls into the lungs—and so goes out of the body as you breathe out.

Bronchioles

The trachea or windpipe
funnels air into the lungs

◀ *Your lungs contain miles of airways
to provide a huge area for oxygen to
seep through into the blood in the
short space of each breath. Breathing
out requires no effort, because the
spongy, elastic material of the lungs
just collapses like a balloon when
you "exhale" (breathe out). But to
breathe in, muscles in the chest
must pull to make the lungs expand.
Intercostal muscles between the ribs
lift the ribcage (the chest's
framework of bone) upward and
outward. At the same time, a domed
sheet of muscle beneath the lung,
called the diaphragm, flattens out,
pulling the lungs down and further
expanding them.*

The diaphragm flattens
to pull the lungs down
and draw air in

DATA: Breathing

- **BREATHS IN A LIFETIME**
  You take about 600 million breaths during your
  lifetime.

- **LUNG AREA**
  Opened out and laid flat, the lungs would cover an
  area the size of a tennis court.

- **LUNG CAPACITY**
  On average, we breathe in and out roughly 2 pints
  (900 ml) of air every ten seconds or so.

- **LENGTH OF AIRWAYS**
  The branching of the bronchioles means that
  altogether there are probably more than 1,500 miles
  (2,400 km) of airways in the lungs!

FACTS: Respiration

- **What is respiration?**
  Respiration not only means
  breathing but also the
  conversion of sugar to energy
  in body cells. This conversion is
  called burning, because it
  creates heat.

- **Aerobic respiration**
  Aerobic respiration is
  when muscle cells
  burn sugar with
  oxygen. Anaerobic
  respiration is when
  they burn sugar
  without oxygen.

▲ *There is not enough
time during a sprint to
boost the oxygen supply
to the muscles, so they
work anaerobically. Only
on longer runs do they
begin to work
aerobically.*

Muscles

EVERY MOVE YOU MAKE–running, dancing, smiling, and everything else–depends on muscles. You even need muscles to sit still: without them, you would slump like a rag doll. Muscles are bundles of fibers that tense and relax to move different parts of the body, and there are two kinds: muscles that you can control, called voluntary muscles, and muscles that you can't, called involuntary muscles. Most voluntary muscles are "skeletal muscles," muscles that move parts of your body when you want to. Involuntary muscles are muscles, such as those of your heart and around your gut, which work automatically.

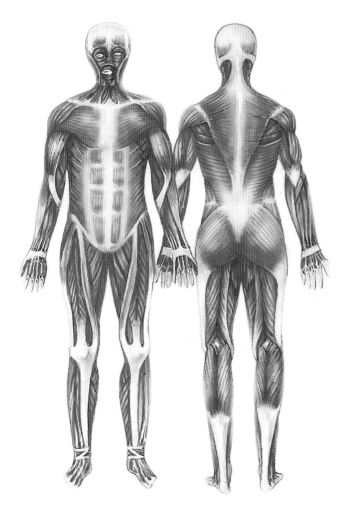

▲ *The body is covered with an almost complete sheath of skeletal muscle pairs, making up 40 percent of the body's weight. There are more than 600 all told, the largest of which is the gluteus maximus in the buttock. In theory, you can control each muscle pair individually. But most work in combinations so well established by habit that they always work together.*

FACTS: About muscles

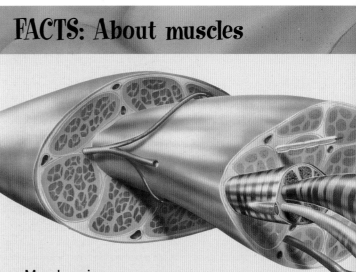

- **Muscle pairs**
  Muscles work by getting shorter, pulling two points together, then relaxing. So most muscles come in pairs: one to pull, the other to pull it back. Typically, there is a "flexor" to bend or flex a joint, and an "extensor" to straighten it again.

- **Muscle fibers**
  Muscles are bundles of fiberlike cells. Some contain just a few hundred, others a quarter of a million or more.

- **Striped strands**
  Most skeletal muscle fibers are made of thin strands called myofibrils. All along the myofibrils are dark and light stripes called striations, which are actually two alternating substances—actin and myosin.

FACTS: About muscles and exercise

- **Red muscle and white muscle**
Slow-twitch "red" muscle fibers are good for prolonged gentle movements. "White" fibers are for short, powerful bursts. Fast-twitch red ones work for both.

◀ *A sportsman trains to develop big muscles, big lungs, and a strong heart.*

- **Oxygen boost**
When muscles work hard they need more oxygen to burn sugar. So when you run your breathing gets faster and deeper, and your heart pumps faster and harder to boost blood supply. Getting in shape develops bigger lungs and a strong heart. If you're not, a long run makes you pant and your heart beat fast.

▼ *In the muscles you use for movement are thousands of long fibers, each made up from hundreds of thinner strands called myofibrils. Alternate bands of actin and myosin filaments in the myofibril give this kind of muscle a stripy or striated look. These filaments interlock and draw together to make the muscle contract.*

▶ *In the upper arm, the biceps at the front is the flexor muscle that contracts (and swells) to bend the arm. The triceps at the back is the extensor that contracts to straighten it out again.*

Muscle made from bundles of muscle fibers

Myofibril made from alternating bands of actin and myosin filament

Muscle fibers are made up from hundreds of myofibrils

Actin filament

Myosin filaments are equipped with hooks like velcro that pull the actin

- **How muscles contract**
In the muscle fibers, filaments of actin and myosin interlock. When the brain sends the muscle a message to contract, little buds on each myosin filament twist sharply, pulling on actin filaments and contracting.

- **Shortening power**
There are millions of actin and myosin filaments in each muscle. When they pull together, they can shorten the muscle by almost half its length.

- **Smooth muscle**
Not all muscles are stripy. Muscles called smooth muscles contract blood vessels to control blood flow to the gut to push food through. The heart is powered by "cardiac" muscle, which beats automatically, although its rate may vary.

Bones

YOUR BODY IS SUPPORTED by a strong frame called the skeleton. The skeleton not only provides an anchor for muscles, but makes a mount for skin and other tissues, and protects the heart, brain, and other organs. It is made of more than 200 bones, linked by a rubbery substance called cartilage. Bones are very tough and light because their outside is made from a mixture of hard minerals, such as calcium, and stringy, elastic collagen. Inside the tough, dry casing, there are holes called lacunae full of living cells called osteocytes, which are bathed in blood-just like every other cell in the body.

FACTS: About joints

- **Moving joints**
  Joints allow the bones of the skeleton to move. The shoulder is a ball and socket joint. The knee and elbow are hinges, like a door hinge. The neck is a swiveling joint, allowing the head to rotate.

- **Spinal joints**
  The joints between backbones are "cartilaginous," joined by layers of cartilage which are stiff but allow a little movement.

- **Knee joints**
  Knee joints are lubricated by capsules of oil called synovial fluid, so are called synovial joints.

◄ Skiing and other sporting activities put a tremendous strain on the knee joints, but the joints are protected by a sleeve of tough collagen fiber and lubricated by synovial fluid.

▼ The skeleton is a strong but remarkably mobile framework. It has two main parts. The main or "axial" part of the skeleton is the skull, spine, ribs, and sternum (breastbone). The bones of the "appendicular" skeleton—arms and legs, along with the shoulders and pelvis (hip bone)—hang from the axial skeleton.

Cranium (skull)

Scapula (shoulder blade)

Humerus (upper arm)

Rib

Sternum (breastbone)

Radius (main forearm)

Ulna (lesser forearm)

FACTS: About bones

- **Fusing bones**
  Babies have more than 300 bones, but many fuse together as they grow, so adults have just 206.

- **Strong bones**
  Weight for weight, bone is five times stronger than steel.

- **Long and short bones**
  The longest, strongest bone is the thigh bone, or femur. The smallest is the stirrup in the middle ear.

- **Bone makeup**
  Bone is made up from a network of collagen (protein) fibers filled with calcium and phosphate.

- **Bone breakers**
  Fresh bone material is constantly being made in cells called osteoblasts. Old bone is broken down by osteoclasts.

- **Bone marrow**
  In the hollow center of the breastbone, ribs, and hips is soft, spongy red "marrow" where red and white blood cells are created. All your bones have this red marrow when you are born, but as you grow older, the marrow of long bones, such as the legs and arms, turns yellow.

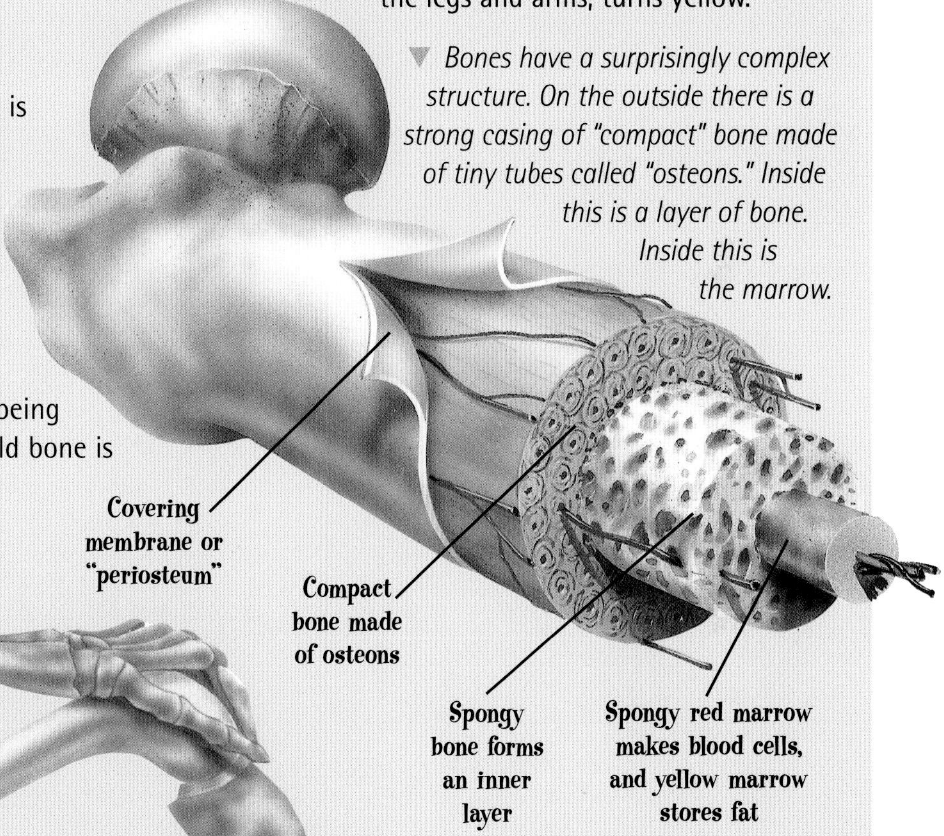

▼ *Bones have a surprisingly complex structure. On the outside there is a strong casing of "compact" bone made of tiny tubes called "osteons." Inside this is a layer of bone. Inside this is the marrow.*

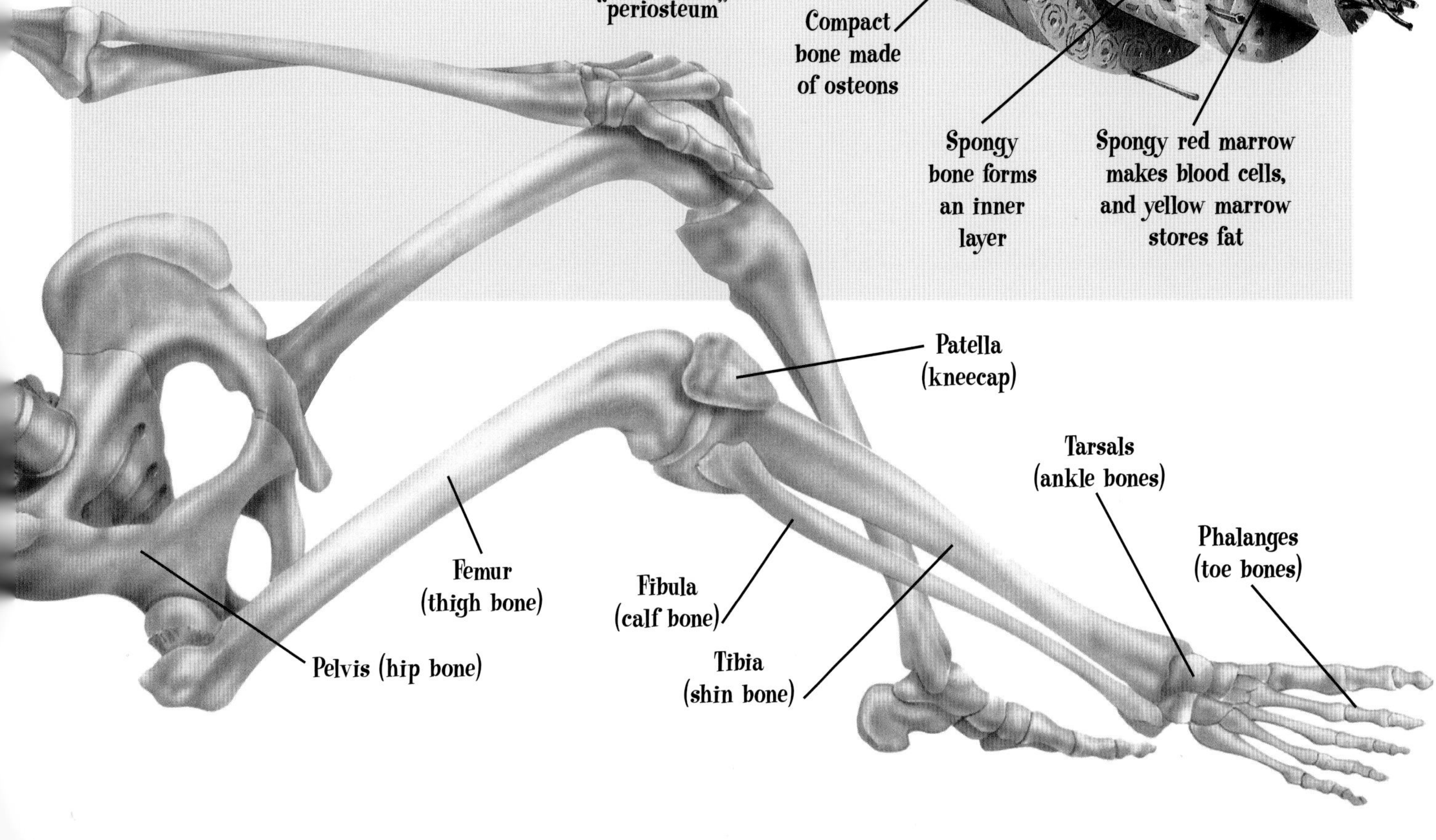

Covering membrane or "periosteum"

Compact bone made of osteons

Spongy bone forms an inner layer

Spongy red marrow makes blood cells, and yellow marrow stores fat

Patella (kneecap)

Tarsals (ankle bones)

Phalanges (toe bones)

Femur (thigh bone)

Fibula (calf bone)

Tibia (shin bone)

Pelvis (hip bone)

Senses

OUR SENSES TELL US what is going on in the world around us. Even when we are asleep, our senses are picking up sensations, some from inside the body, some from outside, and feeding them to the brain via the nerves, which are like the body's telephone wires. We have five main senses to tell us what is going on in the outside world–sight from our eyes, hearing from our ears, smell from our nose, taste from our tongue, and touch from most of our skin. Besides this, there are internal senses, such as pain, and the balance organs in the ear, which tell you whether you are standing upright, or moving fast.

FACTS: About sight

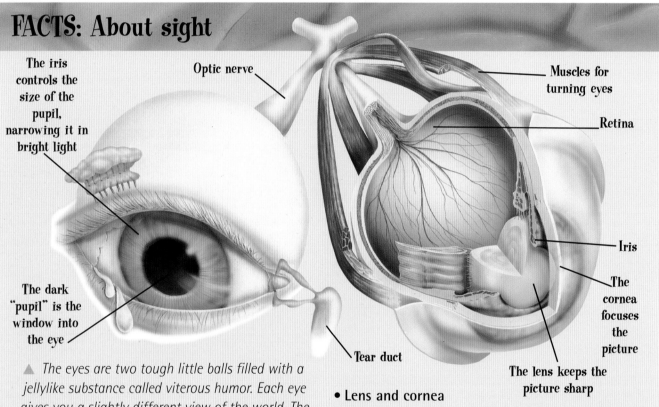

The iris controls the size of the pupil, narrowing it in bright light

Optic nerve

Muscles for turning eyes

Retina

The dark "pupil" is the window into the eye

Iris

The cornea focuses the picture

Tear duct

The lens keeps the picture sharp

▲ The eyes are two tough little balls filled with a jellylike substance called viterous humor. Each eye gives you a slightly different view of the world. The brain combines these different views to give you a complete 3D picture.

• Camera-like eye
Eyes are a bit like video cameras. A lens at the front projects the picture onto the back of the eye, called the retina, where millions of light-sensitive cells detect the picture, and transmit it to the brain via the "optic" nerve.

• Lens and cornea
The eye's main lens is called the cornea, the clear dome in the middle of the eye. The "lens" just behind it changes shape to keep the picture sharp.

• Rods and cones
The light-sensitive cells in the retina are called rods and cones. Rods work even in dim light, but cannot distinguish colors. Cones can distinguish colors, but do not work in dim light, which is why we do not see colors well at night.

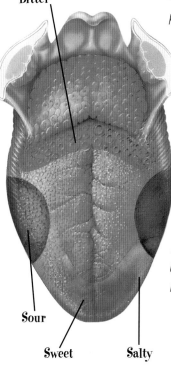

Bitter

Sour

Sweet

Salty

◀ *Smell relies on a small patch of "olfactory" nerves inside the top of your nose which react to minute traces of chemicals in the air. Taste is a mixture of sensations, including smell. But your tongue has four different kinds of taste receptors, called taste buds. They react to sweet, salty, bitter, or sour tastes in food.*

▼ There are touch receptors all over the body, embedded in the skin. They react to four kinds of feeling—a light touch, steady pressure, heat and cold, and pain. Receptors called Meissner's corpuscles are responsible for light touch. Merkel's disks pick up steady pressure.

Cross-section through the skin

Merkel's disk

Meissner's corpuscle

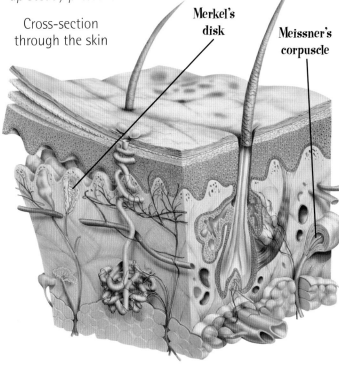

FACTS: About hearing

▼ *The flap of skin on the outside of your head is only one part of the ear, called the outer ear. It just funnels sound down a canal called the ear canal into your head. The real workings of the ear are inside your head. Here are the bones of middle ear, and the curly tube of the inner ear.*

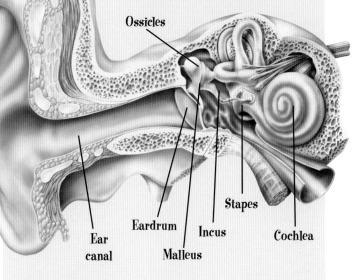

Ossicles

Stapes

Eardrum   Incus   Cochlea

Ear canal   Malleus

- **The middle ear**
  The middle ear is the ear's amplifier. Sound entering the middle ear hits a taut wall of skin called the eardrum, shaking it rapidly. As it shakes, it rattles three tiny bones or "ossicles," called the malleus (hammer), the incus (anvil), and the stapes (stirrup).

- **The inner ear**
  The inner ear is mainly a curly tube full of fluid, called the cochlea. As the ossicles rattle, they knock against this tube, making waves in the fluid. Minute detector hairs waggle in these waves and, as they move, they send signals along nerves to the brain.

- **Two ears**
  Because we have two ears, we can detect where a sound is coming from—by the minute differences in loudness between each ear.

The nerves and brain

INSIDE YOUR HEAD IS THE MOST amazingly complex known structure in the universe: the human brain. It looks like a huge, soggy gray walnut with a wrinkled surface. It is split into two halves and weighs on average about 3 pounds. But within this soggy mass are literally billions of intricately interconnected nerve cells. The chemical and electrical impulses continually shooting through your brain cells produce all your thoughts, and control nearly all your actions–and record every sensation–by signals sent to and fro along the remarkable network of nerves that link your body to the brain like the wires in a computer.

FACTS: About the brain

- **Brain damage**
  Brain cells depend on oxygen in the blood. If the supply is cut off for even a few seconds, a person loses consciousness. If it is cut off any longer, cells die and the brain becomes damaged.

- **Parts of the brain**
  The layout of the brain reflects the way it evolved. As it grew out from the primitive brain stem at the top of the spine, it became more complex, developing first into the hind brain, then the complicated cerebrum.

- **The center of the brain**
  The core of the brain includes the thalamus and brain stem and controls basic functions, such as breathing and heart rate, without your awareness. The hypothalamus here controls hunger and sleeping. Around the thalamus is the limbic system, which makes you angry or upset.

- **The cerebrum**
  The huge wrinkles of the cerebrum wrap around the core of the brain. This is where you think, and complex tasks such as memory, speech, and conscious control of movement go on. All the folds allow a huge number of nerve cells to be squeezed inside the skull.

Cerebrum: thinking, memory, speech, eyesight, hearing, and much more

Limbic system: emotion

Thalamus: relay station

Hypothalamus: hunger, thirst, and sleeping

Pons

Medulla

Brain stem (medulla and pons): heart rate, breathing

Cerebellum: coordination

Spinal cord

▲ Different areas of the brain are associated with different tasks, such as walking or speaking. Some regions, known as sensory areas, receive signals from sense organs. Others, known as motor areas, are the areas that help you to control muscles and enable you to move.

FACTS: About nerve cells

▼ *Nerve cells receive signals from other nerve cells through tiny branches called dendrites and send them out along a thin, winding tail, or axon. At the far end of the axon the signal is sent on to other cells across tiny gaps called synapses.*

Axon

Synapse

Nucleus

Dendrite

Axon of another
nerve cell

- **Nerve cells**
  Nerve cells or "neurons" are long lived, but when they die, they are not replaced by others.

- **Multi link**
  The nervous system is a network of long strings of nerve cells linked together like beads on a string.

- **Neurotransmitters**
  Nerve signals are sent across synapses, the gaps between nerves, by shots of chemicals called neurotransmitters. Different receptors pick up different neurotransmitters.

◀ *Brain scans show scientists what is going on inside a living brain, and so they now know a great deal about the way the brain works. This has helped them identify, for instance, which areas are active when you are speaking.*

DATA: Nerve facts

- **NERVE SPEED**
  The fastest nerve signals travel at 330 feet per second.

- **NERVE LENGTH**
  Axons vary from $\frac{1}{25}$ inch to 40 inches long.

▶ *The network of nerves in the body— called the nervous system—focuses on the Central Nervous System, or CNS. This includes the brain and the spinal cord (the bundle of nerves in the spine). From the CNS, nerves branch out all over the body.*

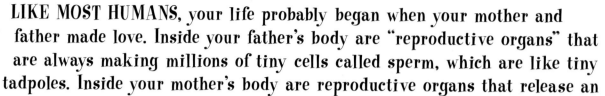

New life

LIKE MOST HUMANS, your life probably began when your mother and father made love. Inside your father's body are "reproductive organs" that are always making millions of tiny cells called sperm, which are like tiny tadpoles. Inside your mother's body are reproductive organs that release an egg into her womb at a certain time every month. Your life began when your mother and father made love at the right time, so that one of your father's sperm worked its way into an egg and fertilized it. The fertilized egg grew gradually inside your mother's womb, until, at last, after nine months or so, you were born.

FACTS: About reproductive organs

- **Puberty**
  You are born with reproductive or sexual organs, but they only develop in the right way for you to have children once you reach the age of puberty—typically 11-13 years. At puberty, chemicals called sex hormones flood through your body, stimulating the changes that turn boys into men and girls into women.

- **Puberty in boys**
  When a boy reaches puberty, his testes grow and begin to produce sperm. At the same time, he begins to grow pubic hair and hair on his chin.

- **Puberty in girls**
  When a girl reaches puberty, she begins to grow breasts, and her monthly periods, or menstruation, start. She, too, grows pubic hair.

- **Menstruation**
  Menstruation is the monthly cycle of changes in a woman's body that prepares her for having a baby. Every four weeks, her ovary releases an egg so that it slides down the Fallopian tube and into her womb. If the egg is not then fertilized, the lining of the womb breaks down and blood flows out of the woman's vagina.

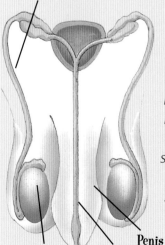

Vas deferens

Testicle   **Urethra**   **Penis**

◄ *In a man's reproductive organs, the sperm is made in the two testes or testicles. When making love, the man's erect penis is inserted into a woman's vagina. When the penis is stimulated enough, a liquid called semen carries the sperm from the testes out through the end of the penis into the vagina.*

Fallopian tube

Ovary

Womb, or uterus

Vagina

◄ *In a woman's reproductive organs, eggs are stored in the two ovaries. One egg is released a month into the womb, or "uterus," via the Fallopian tubes. During love-making, millions of sperm from a man's penis enter the woman's vagina and swim up into the uterus, where only one sperm may penetrate an egg.*

FACTS: About pregnancy

▲ *The moment a sperm enters an egg and fertilizes it is called conception. This is the moment a pregnancy begins. A baby is born about nine months later.*

• **Embryo to fetus**
During the first eight weeks of pregnancy, while internal organs are developing, the new life is called an embryo. After that it is called a fetus (say "feet-us").

• **Lifeline**
The fetus is supplied with oxygen and food via a tube called the umbilical cord. This links the fetus to the placenta, a spongy organ on the womb lining.

DATA: Ova and embryos

• **FERTILE PERIOD**
An egg or ovum can only be fertilized in the 12-24 hours after it is released (called ovulation).

• **GROWING LIFE**
At four weeks, an embryo is no bigger than a grain of rice, but once it becomes a fetus it grows rapidly. At 20 weeks, a fetus is 10 inches long.

The umbilical cord carries the blood supply from the mother that gives the fetus oxygen and food

The placenta is shed after the birth and follows the baby out

After nine months, the baby turns head down, ready to be born

Cervix, known together with the vagina as the birth canal

▲ *In the safety of the mother's womb, the new human life grows from just a few cells to an embryo, then a fetus, to become a baby in nine months, growing larger and more recognizably human by the day. Throughout this time, it is kept warm and cushioned from the outside world inside a bag or sac of fluid called amniotic fluid. When it is ready to be born, the neck of the womb begins to expand, so that the baby can be pushed out through the vagina and into the world.*

Food and waste

BEFORE YOUR BODY CAN USE any of the food you eat, it must be broken down into simple chemical molecules. This is called digestion. It begins the moment you put food in your mouth and chew it until soft. It continues as you swallow the food and it is pushed down the long tube through your body called the alimentary canal, or gut. A barrage of chemicals and squeezing muscles assault the food all the way through the gut until most is ready to be absorbed through the gut and carried to the rest of the body in the blood. Food that cannot be digested goes out through the anus.

FACTS: About waste disposal

- **Cleaning the blood**
  Toxic chemicals and excess water often build up. It is the task of the kidneys to filter these out of the blood and concentrate them into urine.

- **Kidney**
  The kidneys are two bean-shaped organs in the middle of the back. As they filter blood, they regulate body fluid and salt levels and control blood acidity. They filter 15 pints of blood an hour.

- **Ureter and bladder**
  The ureters are the tubes that pipe urine continually from the kidneys to the bladder, a bag where urine builds up until you are able to empty it. The bladder can hold up to a pint of urine.

- **Urethra**
  When you urinate, urine from the bladder drains out of the body through the urethra. This is 8 inches long in men, but just 1 $^1/2$ long in women.

▶ *The kidneys, ureters, bladder, and urethra together make up the urinary system, the body's liquid waste disposal system. Urine is all that is left after valuable ingredients are retrieved by the kidneys from the blood.*

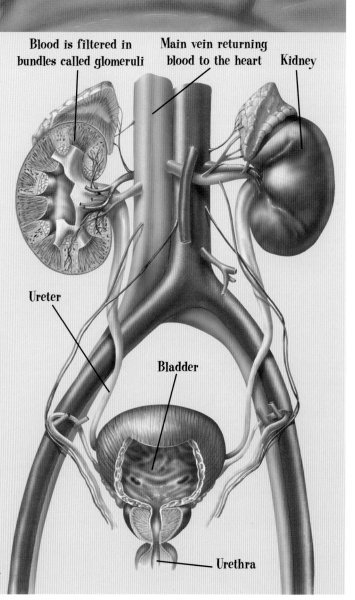

Blood is filtered in bundles called glomeruli

Main vein returning blood to the heart

Kidney

Ureter

Bladder

Urethra

FACTS: About digestion

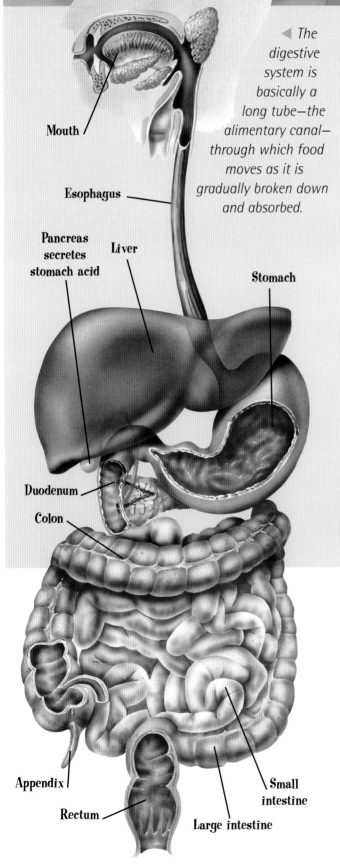

◄ The digestive system is basically a long tube—the alimentary canal—through which food moves as it is gradually broken down and absorbed.

Mouth

Esophagus

Pancreas secretes stomach acid

Liver

Stomach

Duodenum

Colon

Appendix

Rectum

Small intestine

Large intestine

• **The stomach**
Food spends about six hours in the stomach. Here it is churned up by the muscles of the stomach wall and attacked by "gastric" juices, including hydrochloric acid and powerful enzymes, secreted by glands in the stomach wall.

• **Stomach gate**
Food is held in the stomach by a ring of muscle called the pyloric sphincter until it is partly digested.

• **Food names**
A lump of swallowed food is called a bolus. Once partly digested by the stomach it is called chyme.

• **Small intestine**
From the stomach, food goes into the tube called the small intestine, where it is absorbed into the blood. Food undigested here passes into the large intestine, or bowel, where waste is turned solid.

• **Rippling muscles**
Food is moved through the gut by ripples of the muscles in the gut wall. Muscles extend in front of the bolus or chyme and contract behind it to push it along. This is called peristalsis.

• **Liver**
The liver has many functions, including turning digested food into blood proteins.

DATA: Digestion

• **LONG GUT**
Your gut is folded over so many times that it is six times as long as you are tall–up to 33 feet.

• **FOOD IN THE BODY**
Food takes on average 24 hours to pass all the way through the alimentary canal.

The healthy body

THE HUMAN BODY IS REMARKABLY GOOD at taking care of itself, and it has a wide range of mechanisms to help it adjust to different circumstances. But to stay healthy, it needs the right food and regular exercise. Most of the food we eat is fuel burned by the body for energy. But the body also needs small quantities of foods, such as proteins, which are needed to repair cells and build new ones. It also needs minute traces of chemicals that it cannot make for itself: vitamins and minerals. A healthy diet is one that includes all of these foods in just the right proportion and quantity.

FACTS: About diet

• **Foods**
There are three main kinds of food—carbohydrates, fats, and proteins—as well as vitamins, minerals, water, and fiber.

• **Carbohydrates**
Carbohydrates are foods, such as sugars and starches, found in abundance in foods, such as bread, rice, potatoes, and sweet things. They are the body's main source of energy along with fats.

◄ *You need a balanced diet to get the carbohydrates, fats, and protein you need, plus vitamins and minerals, and the fiber needed to take food through the gut properly. A good diet might include fresh fruit and vegetables, brown bread, fish, eggs, cheese, and meat.*

Eating too much carbohydrate-rich and fatty food can cause weight gain. To stay healthy, you should eat these foods in moderate amounts, and exercise regularly to ensure your body is efficient at burning off any excess fat.

FACTS: Vitamins & minerals

- **Vitamins**
Vitamins are chemicals vital for life, found in foods. There are 13 major vitamins: A, C, D, E, K, and 8 varieties of B. Each has a range of tasks in the body. Vitamin C (in citrus fruit) helps fight infection and keep gums and teeth healthy. Vitamin A (found in carrots, green vegetables, and milk) helps keep skin and bones healthy.

- **Essential minerals**
Essential minerals include small amounts of salt, calcium for bones, iron for red blood cells, and tiny traces of minerals, such as iodine.

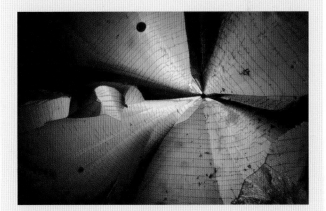

Vitamins are mostly fairly simple chemicals, such as folic acid (one of the B vitamins), but they are vital for life. This picture shows a vitamin crystal in close-up.

- **Fats**
Fats are greasy foods that won't dissolve in water. Some are solid, such as meat fat and cheese. Others, such as corn oil, are liquid. Fats are not only used by the body as energy stores but are a source of vitamins D and E.

- **Too much fat**
Too much fat not only makes you fat. Too much "saturated" fat—mainly animal fat such as butter—can boost the risk of heart disease.

- **Essential acids**
The body needs 20 "amino acids" to build into protein to make and repair cells. The body can make 12 of these; the other eight it must get from protein in food. These are the "essential amino acids."

- **Protein**
Protein in fish and meat has all the amino acids the body needs. Fruit and vegetables have only some of them, which is why vegetarians must choose the right mixture.

- **Protein sources**
Beans and nuts are the most protein-rich foods. The protein content in: soybean flour is 40%; peanuts 28%; cheese 25%; raw meat 23%; raw fish 15%; eggs 12%; bread 8%; rice 6%.

DATA: Food

- **FOOD NEEDS**
On average people need around 2,000 calories of energy food a day.

- **FOOD INTAKE**
On average, people in the United States eat 3,200 calories a day. In Ethiopia, they survive on less than 500 calories a day.

Sickness and disease

EVERY NOW AND THEN, people succumb to sickness and disease. Most diseases, fortunately, are minor, and the ill person usually recovers quickly, thanks to the body's remarkable defense system, called the immune system. Sickness is caused either by an internal failure of one of the body's mechanisms–or by invading microbes or germs. This is where the immune system comes in. The body's immune system not only identifies the germs, but fights them with an array of chemical and biological weapons, including formidable "immune cells." Only the very worst diseases defeat the body's immune system.

FACTS: About the immune system

- **The lymphatic system**
  Lymph is a clear fluid that drains from cells into the bloodstream via a network of capillaries called the lymph system. Immune cells patrol all through the blood, but are concentrated in the lymph system.

- **Inflame response**
  Some germs set off an inflame response. This attacks all germs the same way, increasing blood flow, and bringing a flood of cells called neutrophils into play.

- **Antibodies**
  Antibodies are labels that attach to germs and show killer cells which cells to kill.

- **Killer cells**
  Among the many kinds of immune cells, two kinds of white blood cell are the most important: killer "T" cells, which engulf germs, and B lymphocytes, which identify invaders and make antibodies.

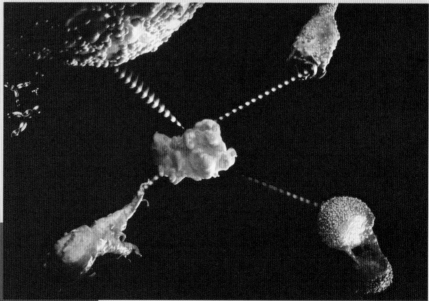

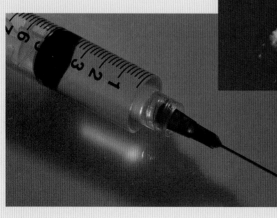

▲ *Invaders are targeted by the body's immune system in a number of ways to ensure they are beaten off.*

◄ *Vaccination is designed to trigger the body to make antibodies against a disease.*

FACTS: About germs

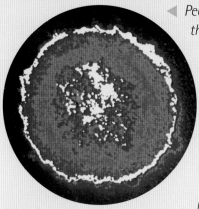

◄ *People infected with the HIV virus often succumb to the deadly disease AIDS. This virus is deadly because it attacks the body's immune system and renders it ineffective.*

• **Infection**
Many germs cause infection, when bacteria, viruses, or fungi multiply within your body. As they multiply they either damage cells directly, as viruses do, or may release harmful toxins.

• **Fever and inflammation**
Infection activates the immune system, and many of the symptoms you feel—fever, weakness, inflammation—are side-effects of the immune system's struggle.

• **Bacteria and viruses**
Viruses are very tiny and can only multiply by entering other cells—such as your body's cells—and taking them over. Bacteria are much bigger—they are tiny one-celled organisms.

DATA: Immune cells

• **ANTIBODY NUMBERS**
There are thousands of different antibodies in the blood, each targeted against a particular "antigen" (invader).

• **GIANT EATER**
A single "macrophage" (giant eater) T cell can eat up to 100 bacteria.

▼ *Unlike viruses, bacteria can multiply outside the body and can be grown in dishes of protein to create "cultures." By growing cultures, scientists can test antibiotic drugs on them and see which are the most effective at killing them off.*

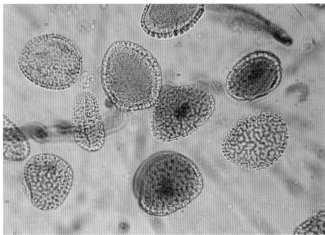

▲ *A common form of allergy is hay fever. In the summer, grasses and other plants release pollen. When this is inhaled, it can cause allergic reactions in some people, such as streaming eyes and sneezing.*

31

What's wrong?

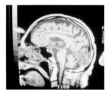

BEFORE YOU CAN BE TREATED for any illness or injury, the doctor has to decide just what is wrong. This is called diagnosis. The most important clues for a diagnosis are usually the symptoms–that is, all the signs that something may be wrong–a cough, a rash, a pain in your side, and so on. The doctor may also find clues in the story of events that led up to the illness, called the history. The illness or injury can often be identified from the symptoms and history alone. If not, you may have to undergo various tests, or have pictures taken of your insides with X-rays or scanners.

FACTS: Looking for clues

- **History**
  Most visits to the doctor begin with the history. While you tell the doctor your symptoms, he or she asks you other questions about the course of events, takes notes, and begins to form an idea about the nature of the problem.

- **The examination**
  The doctor may then go on to look at and listen to the appropriate parts of your body where he thinks there may be further clues. This is called the physical examination. A doctor may look at your eyes using a device called an opthalmoscope, for instance, or tap on your stomach to hear if the taps vibrate through your internal organs normally. He may also check your temperature or blood pressure.

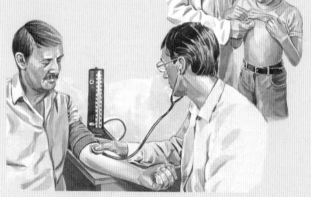

In the physical examination, the doctor may listen to your chest (right) or check your blood pressure (below).

- **Listening to the chest**
  The doctor can tell a great deal just by listening to your chest using a stethoscope. A stethoscope is a simple listening tube. The tight membrane picks up slight sounds inside your body and the tube transmits them to the doctor's ears. Stethoscopes are particularly important for any problems connected with your breathing or heart.

Athletes continually monitor their bodies– whether they are ill or not–to check that they are achieving peak performance.

FACTS: About CT and other scans

- **CT scans**
  CT, or Computerized Tomography, scans use computers to build up a series of pictures showing slices through the body.

- **How CT works**
  Inside a CT scanner, an X-ray gun rotates around the patient, firing as it goes. Light detectors on the far side pick up the rays. A computer analyzes what happened to each ray as it passed through the patient's body to build up a detailed picture.

- **MRI scans**
  MRI or Magnetic Resonance Imaging uses a powerful magnet to line up all the protons (tiny atomic particles) in a patient's body. A brief pulse of radio waves then knocks them briefly out of alignment. As they snap back into alignment afterward, they send out little radio signals themselves. The scanner picks up all these billions of tiny signals to give a detailed picture of the body inside.

▼ CT scans are especially good at showing deep inside the brain and have revolutionized the treatment of head injuries.

The X-ray gun rotates around the porthole firing low-dose X-ray beams

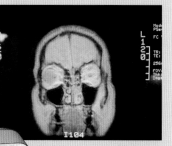

◀ For a CT scan, the patient lies on a moving bed and slides into a porthole in the scanner.

FACTS: About X-rays

- **X-rays**
  X-rays are a simple and effective way of taking a black and white picture of the inside of your body.

  ▶ This is an X-ray of someone's chest. The ribcage shows up clearly as pale, curved bars.

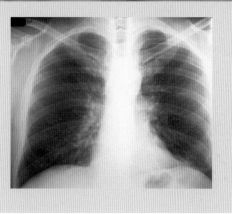

- **X-rays**
  X-rays are a bit like light, but they are made from waves too short to see—and they can pass straight through certain tissues in your body to turn photographic film black. Tissues that block their path show up white on film.

Treatments and cures

YOUR BODY HAS ITS OWN RANGE OF defenses against illness, called the immune system, and it can fight off many diseases unaided if you are in pretty good shape. But doctors have many treatments to help when the immune system cannot cope. Some are so effective that many illnesses that were once inevitably fatal, such as tuberculosis, can often now be treated with drugs. Many diseases can be prevented by vaccination programs, that make the most of the body's immune system. Germs-little organisms such as bacteria and viruses that cause illness-can also be kept at bay by proper hygiene.

FACTS: About drugs

- **Antibiotics**
  Many illnesses that are caused by bacteria can be treated with drugs called antibiotics. These were originally made from molds and fungi, but are now made synthetically. They include penicillin and tetracycline.

- **How drugs are made**
  In the past, drugs mostly came from natural substances. Now most are made in the laboratory or designed on computer. A few drugs are made by manipulating the genes of living organisms so that they produce the drug. Insulin, for instance, is made in the pancreas of pigs or oxen.

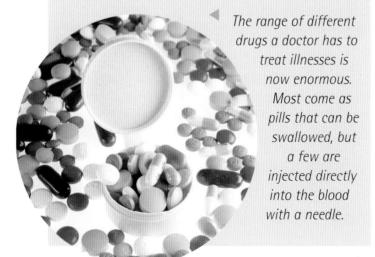

The range of different drugs a doctor has to treat illnesses is now enormous. Most come as pills that can be swallowed, but a few are injected directly into the blood with a needle.

FACTS: About vaccination

▶ This is the germ that causes the terrible disease AIDS, magnified tens of thousands of times. The germ is a virus that attacks the body's immune system. Doctors are looking for a vaccine against it.

▼ Most children have vaccinations at regular intervals as they grow up against diseases, such as diphtheria, whooping cough, and tetanus.

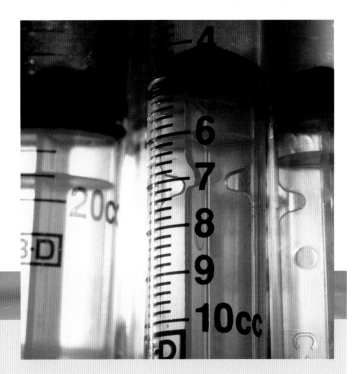

▲ Many vaccines are made by genetic engineering—that is, by altering the genes of the germ to make it harmless. These are called live attenuated organisms.

- **Disease protection**
  You can be protected from some diseases by immunization or vaccination.

- **Passive immunization**
  For immediate, short-lived protection from an infection, you might be injected with blood from someone who has already survived the disease. The blood contains tiny proteins called antibodies, which defend your body against the invading germ.

- **Active immunization**
  For long term protection, you may be injected with a killed or mild version of the germ. Your body then makes its own antibodies against the germ, and so is resistant to further infection.

- **Killing diseases**
  Many once common diseases—diphtheria, polio, measles, and whooping cough—are now quite rare thanks to mass vaccination of children. Smallpox is now very rare indeed.

▶ The way ordinary hospitals and doctors treat illnesses is based on science and is called conventional medicine. But there are many alternative approaches. Some are based on traditional methods passed down from generation to generation over thousands of years. Many people in Africa go to a witch doctor (right). Other alternatives include herbal medicine, which uses herbs as treatments, and Chinese acupuncture, which uses needle pricks in carefully chosen places.

▼ When people are sick, proper care may be as important as the right medicines. If you are only mildly sick, your family or friends can look after you. In hospital, you may be tended by nurses, who make sure you are taking medicines correctly and provide the right food and fluids.

Body repairs

SOMETIMES, WHEN YOUR BODY cannot heal itself, or when treatment with drugs is inappropriate, the only solution may be to cut it open and physically repair it, just as you would a broken-down automobile. This is called surgery. Surgeons might cut open your body to cut out a diseased or wrongly functioning organ, such as your appendix, or mend a broken bone. They might also, if you are very ill, take out an organ from your body and replace it with a healthy organ from another person (maybe from someone who has died). This is called a transplant.

FACTS: About surgery

• **Local anesthetic**
A minor operation is generally done under a local anesthetic. This means a drug is wiped on the skin or injected to numb any feeling in just the area being operated on.

• **General anesthetic**
Major operations are done under a general anesthetic. This means the patient is given a drug by injection, or breathes a gas that sends him or her to sleep for the entire operation. You would need a general anesthetic to have a heart transplant or to have your appendix out.

▲ In a heart transplant, a diseased heart is cut out and replaced with a healthy heart from someone who has died.

• **Organ transplants**
All these parts of the body may be transplanted: kidney, cornea of the eye; the heart, heart and lungs; the liver; and the pancreas.

• **Transplanted organs**
After a transplant, the body's immune system may reject the new organ as foreign. So the patient is given drugs to suppress the immune system.

◀ Major surgery involves a team of people working together in a specially equipped room called an operating room. The team is headed by the surgeon but also involves an anesthetist and nurses.

FACTS: About implants and prosthetics

- **Implants**
  Sometimes, damaged or diseased parts inside the body, such as the hip bone, may be replaced by special-purpose parts made of materials, such as metal and nylon. These are called implants.

- **Pacemakers**
  People with heart problems, for instance, may be given a pacemaker, a tiny electronic device that sends out electrical signals to the heart muscles to keep the heart beating steadily.

- **Prosthetics**
  Prosthetics are artificial parts attached to the outside of the body. Someone who has lost an arm, for instance, may be given an artificial one, complete with hinged elbow and movable fingers.

▶ *Implants have to be made of tough, noncorrosive material. This illustration shows parts of the body that may be replaced by implants made of the metal titanium—the same tough, shiny metal that is often used in aircraft.*

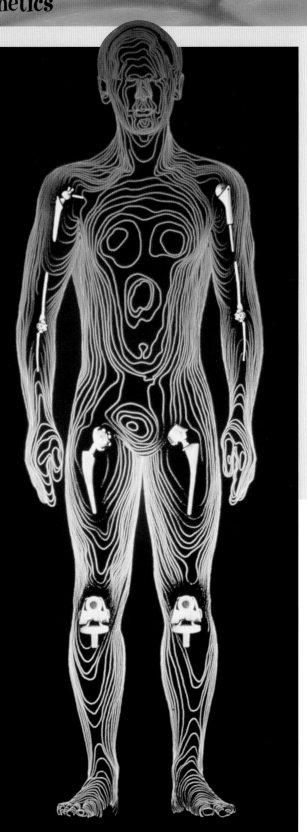

▼ *Using a microscope, a microsurgeon can carry out operations on a minute scale—to connect fine blood vessels in the eye or to rejoin minute nerves and tendons severed in an injury.*

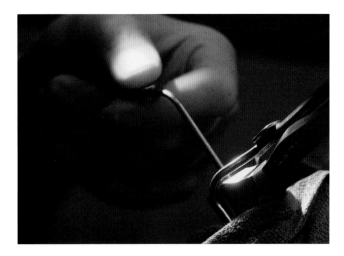

Key facts: People

People: tallest, shortest, oldest, youngest

- The tallest man ever was the American Robert Wadlow (b. 1918) who reached 8 feet, 11 inches tall.
- The shortest man ever was Gul Mohammed from India (1957–97), who was just 22 inches tall when examined in 1990.
- The fattest man ever was American Jon Minnoch, who weighed 1,400 pounds when he died in 1983.
- The lightest human adult ever was the Mexican girl Lucia Xarate who weighed about 4.7 pounds when she was 17 in 1889.
- There is a woman in Africa who is thought to have lived to 150 years old, but no one can prove it.
- In 1997, Frenchwoman Jeanne Calment died aged 122 years and 164 days.
- In 1986, Japanese Shigechiyo Izumi died aged 120 years and 237 days.
- The most children born at once were decaplets—2 boys and 8 girls born in 1946 in Bacacy in Brazil.
- Mr. and Mrs. Vassileyev, who lived near Moscow in 1782, had 69 of their own children.

Inside the body

- There are more than 600 billion cells in your body.
- There are more than 200 types of cell in your body.
- There are 100 billion nerve cells in your brain.
- 14% of your body weight is bone; 40% is muscle.
- You have 213 bones in your body.
- Babies have 300 bones.
- There are 22 bones in your skull.
- There are 33 bones or vertebrae in your spine.
- You have 7 pairs of true ribs, 3 false ribs and 2 floating ribs.
- There are 27 bones in your hand.
- The longest bone is the femur or thighbone.
- You have 640 muscles in your body.
- The longest muscle is the sartorius on the inside of the thigh.
- The biggest muscle in your body is the gluteus maximus or buttock.

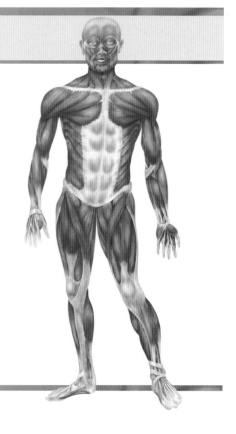

Breath facts

- You will probably take about 600 million breaths if you live to the age of 75.
- Every minute you are alive, you breathe in more than 200 fluid ounces of air.
- A normal breath takes in about 14 fluid ounces of air.
- On average, you breathe about 13-17 times a minute.
- If you run hard, you may have to breathe up to 80 times a minute.

- Newborn babies breathe about 40 times a minute.
- There are about 300 million little air sacs, or alveoli, in your body.
- Opened out and laid flat, your lungs would cover an area about the size of a tennis court.
- There are more than 1,500 miles of airways in your lungs.

Blood count

- Your heart beats 30 million times each year.
- The chambers of the heart each hold about 2 $\frac{1}{2}$ fluid ounces of blood.
- Pulse rates average 60 to 100 beats a minute.
- Blood travels through the capillaries at 3 feet a second.
- There are 36,000 miles of capillary in your body.
- Capillaries may be just a thousandth of an inch thick.
- Someone who weighs 165 pounds has about 11 pints of blood.

- Someone who weighs 165 pounds and lives on the high Andes has about 13 pints of blood.
- A microliter of blood holds 4-6 million red blood cells.
- A microliter of blood holds 5-10,000 white blood cells.
- A microliter of blood holds 150,000-500,000 platelets.
- Blood is 60% plasma.
- Plasma is 90% water.
- There are 13 blood clotting factors, numbers I-XIII.
- There are 4 blood groups: A, O, N, and ABO.
- 85% belong to the blood type Rhesus positive.

Milestones

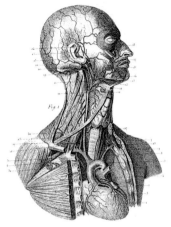

- 1543: Vesalius created his book *De Humani Corporis Fabrica*—which became the basis of modern anatomy.
- 1550: Gabriel Fallopio's close study of the body revealed tiny structures.
- 1590: Santorio Sanctorius created the science of physiology. He also showed how to measure pulse and temperature.
- 1628: William Harvey revealed how the heart circulates blood.
- 1661: Using a microscope, Marcello Malphigi saw tiny blood vessels called capillaries.
- 1798: Edward Jenner showed people could be vaccinated against infectious diseases.
- 1840s: Rudolf Virchow and Jakob Henle found that the body is built up from tissues made from tiny cells.
- 1900: Karl Landsteiner showed that people's blood belongs to different groups.

Key facts: People

- 1906: Frederick Hopkins suggested the existence of vitamins and that a lack of them caused scurvy and rickets.
- 1920s: Charles Best and Frederick Banting discovered how to control diabetes with insulin.
- 1923: First vaccine for Diphtheria.
- 1927: First vaccine for Tuberculosis.
- 1928: Alexander Fleming accidentally discovered penicillin.
- 1935: First vaccine for Yellow Fever.
- 1940: Howard Florey and Ernst Chain developed penicillin as a working antibiotic.
- 1951: The heart-lung machine was invented.
- 1963: An oral vaccine against polio became available for use.
- 1967: Christiaan Barnard performed the first human heart transplant.
- 1978: Birth of Louise Brown, the first "test-tube" baby.
- 1980: Smallpox was eradicated worldwide.
- 2003: The Human Genome Project was completed. All the genes in human DNA were identified.
- 2005: The World Health Organization warned of a possible flu pandemic resulting from bird flu mutations.

Record feats

- The longest period of hiccuping, by American Charles Osborne, lasted for 68 years (1922–1990).
- The world's biggest feet belong to American Matthew McGrory. His feet are size 29.5 (size 29 UK shoes, size 63 European shoes).
- The longest extension of a human neck is 15 $^3/4$ inches by the Padaung women of Myanmar.

- The longest interval between the birth of two children to the same mother is 41 years 185 days. Elizabeth Ann Buttle's first child was born in 1956, and the last in 1997, when she was aged 60.
- The shortest interval between two children born to separate confinements is 208 days, by Jayne Bleackley. She gave birth to her son on September 3, 1999, and to her daughter on March 30, 2000.
- The oldest human footprints discovered date back 117,000 years. They were found in South Africa.
- The longest fit of sneezing lasted 978 days, by 12-year-old English girl Donna Griffiths.
- The most blood donated was 41$^1/2$ gallons by Maurice Creswick of South Africa.

Body's ingredients

Chemical element	Proportion of total weight (%)	Ounces in average adult body
Oxygen	65	1,373
Carbon	18.5	391
Hydrogen	9.5	201
Nitrogen	3.2	68
Calcium	1.5	32
Phosphorus	1	21
Potassium	0.4	8.5
Sulfur	0.3	6
Chlorine	0.2	4
Sodium	0.2	4
Magnesium	0.1	2

Other main elements: iodine, iron, cobalt, copper, fluorine, manganese, zinc, silicon

B boron 5	C carbon 6	N nitrogen 7	O oxygen 8	F fluorine 9
Si silicon 14	P phosphorus 15	S sulphur 16	Cl chlorine 17	
As arsenic 33	Se selenium 34	Br bromine 35		
Te tellurium 52	I iodine 53			
At astatine 85				

Classification: - humans

Kingdom:	Animals
Phylum:	Chordates
Subphylum:	Vertebrates
Class:	Mammals
Order:	Primates—lemurs, bushbabies, monkeys, and apes
Family:	Hominids—humans and their close relatives
Genus:	Homo "human"
Species:	Homo sapiens "wise human." All human beings are in this group.

Brain facts

• The brain has three main parts:
1) the cerebrum is where thinking and memory take place.
2) the cerebellum coordinates muscular activity, such as walking.
   3) the brain stem controls involuntary activity, such as breathing.

• Each half (or hemisphere) of the brain works slightly differently:

Left brain
• right-handed skills
• speech
• language, reading, and writing
• math
• logic and reasoning

Right brain
• left-handed skills
• creating music
• sculpture, arts, spatial awareness (patterns and shapes)
• imagination and ideas
• visual imagery

Quiz: People

1. Vitamin C helps your body fight infection. Which foods are particularly rich in vitamin C?

2. On average, how many calories of energy from food do people need every day?

3. How much air do we breathe in and out every 10 seconds?

4. Blood carries food as well as oxygen to the body cells: true or false?

5. Your pulse–the rate your heart beats–is normally 300 beats a minute: true or false?

6. What are the major blood vessels that carry blood out (away) from the heart called?

7. The tiniest blood vessels are called capillaries: true or false?

8. Your biggest muscle is in your buttocks: true or false?

9. How many muscles do you have in your body–640 or 1,170?

10. What are the muscles at the front of the upper arm called?

11. Which is the longest bone in your body?

12. What is the name of the spongy red substance in the hollow center of the breastbone, ribs, and hips?

13. What is the colored part of your eye called?

14. The back part of the eye, where the image is projected, is called the retina: true or false?

15. The curly tube in your inner ear is called the cockle: true or false?

16. The taste buds on your tongue can detect four different kinds of tastes: salty, bitter, sour, and one other—what is it?

17. The brain is the only part of the body that can survive without oxygen: true or false?

18. When nerve cells die, they are not replaced by others: true or false?

19. The tallest man who ever lived grew to be 8 feet 11 inches tall: true or false?

20. What is the name of the tiny electronic device fitted inside people with heart problems?

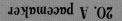

Answers:

1. Citrus fruit
2. 2,000
3. 2 pints
4. True
5. False—it is 60-100 beats a minute
6. Arteries
7. True
8. True—the gluteus maximus is your biggest muscle
9. 640
10. Biceps
11. Your thighbone or femur
12. Marrow
13. The iris
14. True
15. False—it is called the cochlea
16. Sweet
17. False—even a few minutes without oxygen damages the brain
18. True
19. True
20. A pacemaker

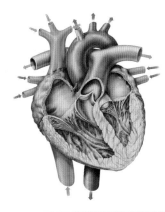

ANIMALS

Small mammals

MAMMALS COME IN ALL SHAPES AND SIZES and live in a huge variety of places, from the frozen arctic wastes to the hottest desert. Like fish, birds, amphibians, and reptiles, they are "vertebrates"-animals with backbones. This really means they have a bony skeleton inside their bodies, which makes a strong frame for hanging everything on. Besides a backbone, mammals usually have two pairs of limbs, a skull to hold the brain, eyes, ears, and a nose-and then a heart, lungs, and guts inside the ribs.

FACTS: About mammals

- **Warm-blooded**
  Mammals are said to be endothermic (warm-blooded) and reptiles exothermic (cold-blooded). This doesn't mean reptiles' blood is necessarily colder. It just means that mammals are able to keep their blood and bodies equally warm all the time—which is why they can survive in so many different places.

- **Babies**
  All mammals begin life as a tiny egg inside their mother's body. But most young mammals develop inside their mother's body until they are born as babies. Very few baby mammals can cope by themselves when they are born, and most need looking after by their parents for while. Human babies need looking after for many years.

- **Mammals that lay eggs**
  A few mammals living in Australia called monotremes lay eggs rather than have babies. These include the duck-billed platypus.

- **Milk power**
  Unlike other animals, mother mammals feed their babies on milk until they are old enough to cope with solid foods. Milk gives all the fat and protein the baby needs to grow.

- **Milk on tap**
  The more babies a mother mammal tends to have, the more pairs of teats she has. Humans have just one pair, but pigs have seven pairs.

- **Big and small**
  The biggest mammal is the blue whale, 100 feet long and weighing 330,000 pounds; the smallest land mammal is the Etruscan shrew, smaller than your thumb and weighing only 1/16 ounce.

- **Fur coats**
  All mammals have a fur coat, even if it is just made up of a few strands like with humans, rhinos, and whales. Fur keeps the animal warm by trapping a layer of insulating air.

- **Clever creatures**
  Compared to other animals, much more of a mammal's brain is cerebrum, the part of the brain devoted to intelligent behavior. In humans and apes, the proportion is biggest of all.

◀ The badger is one of 4,200 known species of mammal around the world.

FACTS: About rodents

- **Rodents**
  There are more than 1,700 species of rodent, including rats and mice, rabbits, and guinea pigs.

- **Front teeth**
  All rodents have two pairs of ever-growing, razor-sharp front teeth, or incisors, for gnawing.

▲ *Porcupines are small mammals covered in incredibly long spines, which protect them from predators. When threatened, they rustle or rattle their spines—or even run backward into the enemy, spines pointing.*

◀ *Squirrels have fur-lined cheek pouches, which they use for storing food.*

▲ *Weasels are among the most effective of all small predators— they are both agile and strong.*

▶ *Beavers are the biggest of all rodents, except for the South American capybara. They live in water and use their sharp teeth to gnaw through trees to get wood to dam streams. They build their homes, called lodges, in the pond created behind this dam.*

The inside of the beaver's lodge is above water level, but it is reached by an underwater entrance

Beavers have two very sharp teeth for gnawing

Beavers' big flat tails and webbed back feet make them good swimmers

Large mammals

SOME MAMMALS ARE TINY but the big mammals are the biggest living things in the world. The biggest of all the mammals on land are elephants, which can grow up to 13 feet tall—twice as tall as a basketball player—and weigh 15,500 pounds, which is as much as a big truck. Not that much smaller are two other creatures of tropical Africa and Asia, the rhinoceros and hippopotamus. All of these big mammals are herbivores, which means they eat plants. So, too, are the many medium-size herd animals, such as buffalos and horses.

FACTS: About elephants

- **Long nose**
  An elephant's most remarkable feature is its long trunk, or "proboscis," which it uses for breathing, smelling, pulling down branches, picking up objects, making trumpeting noises, and for sucking up water.

- **Long life**
  Elephants live longer than all mammals apart from man, surviving up until the age of 80 in captivity.

- **Big ears**
  When an elephant holds its ears back flat, it is either relaxed, or feeling cowed by another. A dominant or aggressive bull (male elephant) often sticks its ears out.

- **Big teeth**
  Elephants have two giant teeth called tusks, which they use for digging or to fend off enemies. Bulls sometimes lock tusks and wrestle with their trunks to see who's strongest.

- **Keeping cool**
  To cool off in the heat, elephants stretch out or flap their ears. They also cover themselves with mud or spray themselves with dust or water. Coating their skin like this also helps to condition their skin and provide a protective layer.

- **Herds**
  Elephants live in herds, ranging from four to 30 members, led by a mature cow, or "matriarch." The rest of a herd is generally made up of several females and their young, as well as a few young bulls. Adult males tend to move off and live on their own or in all male groups.

Tusks curve as they grow

▶ *Elephants in Africa are much bigger than those found in Asia, with an African bull weighing up to 15,500 pounds.*

Rhinos, such as this Indian rhinoceros, have thick, hairless skin, which is arranged like protective armor, folding at the neck, shoulders, and legs to allow movement. Some species of rhino also have one horn; some have two. These horns are actually made of densely compacted hair, or "keratin."

The African elephant has much bigger ears than an Indian elephant, and a sloping forehead instead of a domed one.

Horses belong to a group of mammals called ungulates, or hooved mammals. As with pigs, cattle, and camels, claws have been replaced with hooves. Each foot of a horse has one toe with a toenail, which is the hoof. They are very fast runners, using just the tip of this toe as they move.

FACTS: About herbivores

- **Grazers and browsers**
  Herbivores that eat grasses are called "grazers," while those that eat leaves, bark, and the buds of trees and bushes are called "browsers." Some animals only eat one kind of plant, but most will actually eat a variety, depending on whatever is available.

- **Steady eating**
  Because plants are not as nutritious as meat, most herbivores need to spend large amounts of time eating—unlike carnivores, which feed only occasionally. An elephant, for example, usually feeds for at least 18 hours every day.

The takin (right) is a herbivore that lives in Central Asia. It looks a bit like a goat, but with shorter horns and a stockier body, covered in dense brown hair.

DATA: Large mammals

- **THE BIGGEST ANIMALS**
  Rhinos and hippos are the second heaviest land mammals after elephants. An African white rhinoceros weighs up to 10 tons.

- **AN ELEPHANT'S DIET**
  Elephants eat up to 330 pounds of food per day. They also drink about 50 gallons of water a day.

- **HORSE BREEDS**
  There are 150 different breeds of domestic horse.

Big cats

LIONS, TIGERS, JAGUARS, PUMAS, AND LEOPARDS are kinds of big cats, found all over the world except Australasia. Although they have the same basic body structure as pet cats, they are very different in other ways. They vary in size considerably, from the big tiger to the tiny wild cat, but big cats are usually much bigger and stronger than pet cats, and they roar and grunt rather than meow and purr. All are deadly hunters, slinking up on their prey then pouncing on it. Their sharp claws, powerful jaws, and fangs inflict terrible wounds on victims.

FACTS: About tigers

• **Very big cat**
Tigers are the largest of the big cats, with huge heads and growing 8 feet long. The long tail adds another 3 feet.

• **Disguising stripes**
Tigers are instantly recognizable by their stripes. But in the forest areas of southern Asia where they live, their black stripes on a gold background act as camouflage. Their chins and stomachs are snowy white.

• **Head hunter**
Tigers prey on large animals, such as deer, buffalo, antelopes, and wild pigs, hunting mainly at night. But it takes a tiger a lot of effort to make a kill; nine out of ten times, the victim will actually make a getaway.

• **Endangered tigers**
Hunters killing tigers for their skins, and farmers clearing the forest for land, have decimated tiger numbers, and they are now restricted to special reserves in Asia, mainly in India and Sumatra.

• **Lone males**
Tigers have their own ranges but a male's may include that of some females. They meet only to mate.

• **Young tigers**
Two to four tiger cubs are born at a time and live with their mother for three years as they learn to survive.

▶ Tigers are solitary creatures, living alone most of their lives. To keep other tigers out of their territory, they leave urine samples and scratch marks on trees.

FACTS: About lions

A male can be up to around 10 feet long from his nose to the tip of his tail. Males also have a mane, which gets darker as they get older. Females have no mane and are also a bit smaller.

• **King of the beasts**
Lions are majestic big cats once found all over southern Asia but now found mainly on the grasslands of Africa. They are the only truly social cats, living together in groups called prides. The adult male lion is instantly recognizable by the big mane that covers its head.

• **What lions eat**
Lions feed on wildebeest, zebras, and antelopes—occasionally giraffes. They have big side teeth and short, strong jaws for eating flesh.

• **Lions on the hunt**
It is usually the female that hunts, alone or in pairs, although the males are the first to eat once the prey has been caught. The hunting lionesses stealthily approach a victim then make a short dash and pounce on it quickly. If they don't succeed in their short dash, they give up and wait for another opportunity. Only one in four hunts leads to a kill.

• **A quiet life**
A lion spends 18 hours a day sleeping, because the meat it eats is so nutritious. It eats one solid meal, then goes without food for the next few days.

Among the many smaller big cats is the margay, which lives in the forests of South and Central America and preys on small mammals and birds. The margay is solitary, has good reflexes, keen eyesight, and is an excellent climber. However, it has been hunted for its coat and as a result is now quite rare.

With its spotted coat, the jaguar is one of the most beautiful of the big cats. It lives in South American forests, usually near water, and hunts peccaries, capybaras, and fish. It looks a bit like the leopard of Africa and Asia, but these have black blotches or rings, whereas jaguars have spots with rings around them.

Monkeys and apes

HUMANS, APES, MONKEYS, AND LEMURS all belong to a group of animals called primates. Most of them, except humans, live in places where there are trees, and have hands with fingers, and feet with toes for gripping branches. The apes are our closest relatives in the animal world and have similar long arms, and fingers and toes for gripping. Monkeys have long arms, too, but they are usually much smaller, and have a tail for helping them to balance as they swing through the trees. They live all over the world in warm regions.

FACTS: About lemurs and langurs

- **What are lemurs?**
  Lemurs are nocturnal animals with big, staring eyes. They have soft, thick fur and bushy tails, which they use to intimidate other animals, signal to other lemurs, and wave scent around (from glands in their behinds).

- **Where lemurs live**
  Nearly all lemurs live in forests on the island of Madagascar off the east coast of Africa. They tend to live mostly in trees.

- **Kinds of lemur**
  There are 21 species of lemur. Some are brightly colored, such as the ring-tailed lemur, which has black and white rings all the way down its tail.

- **Tiny primates**
  Lemurs are all quite small— the biggest is only as big as a large house cat, while the smallest, the lesser mouse lemur, grows to only 5 inches.

- **Langurs**
  Langurs are small monkeys that live in Southeast Asia and mainly eat leaves.

▷ *Like other langurs, the Hanuman langur has a strong stomach that can cope with the toughest leaves.*

◁ *Monkeys are divided into those of the Old World and the New World. Old World monkeys, such as the baboon (left), live in the warmer parts of Africa and Asia. They tend to be larger than New World monkeys but do not have prehensile tails (tails that grip). Their backsides are usually naked and their nostrils are close together.*

◁ *New World monkeys live in Central and South American forests. Many, such as the spider monkey (left), have prehensile tails to help them climb and to hang from branches, keeping their legs and arms free for holding food. Their noses are also much wider than those of Old World monkeys and their nostrils face outward.*

FACTS: About apes

- **Fellow apes**
  Apes are so closely related to humans that some zoologists divide apes into three kinds—lesser apes (gibbons and siamangs), great apes (orangutans, gorillas, and chimpanzees) and man. None has a tail.

- **Great apes and lesser apes**
  Great apes are almost human-shaped, although they tend to have longer arms, big, protruding jaws—and, of course, are covered in fur. They are often very clever, too, especially chimpanzees. Lesser apes are smaller and less clever, but they can be be very agile climbers.

- **Chimpanzees**
  Chimps are man's closest relative and the brightest of the apes. They communicate with varied vocal sounds, gestures, and facial expressions. They also use tools, such as sticks, to get food.

- **Gibbons**
  Gibbons are agile apes which live in Southeast Asian forests and swing swiftly from branch to branch—up to 10 feet in a single swing.

- **Orangutan**
  Orangutan is Malay for "old man of the forest." They live in the rain forests of Borneo and Sumatra and look like hairy old men.

Gorillas are the biggest of the apes. A big male can be 68 inches tall. They look ferocious, but are among the gentlest of creatures. They eat only berries and leaves, and the male only becomes aggressive when a rival male intrudes on his group—even then he only beats his chest and roars.

Adult males are called silverbacks because they have gray hairs on their backs

The gentle gorilla only roars like this when his family is threatened

Pandas, bears & dogs

ALL BIG CARNIVOROUS (MEAT-EATING) ANIMALS are essentially either cats or dogs. Cats are very obviously cats, but the dogs include bears, as well as the more obviously doglike creatures, such as wolves, foxes, jackals, and coyotes. To a zoologist, a bear is rather like a big dog without a tail. Both bears and dogs are mostly hunters that eat meat, but unlike cats, bears especially will also eat other things if food is scarce. Surprisingly, although pandas look like bears, they are actually more closely related to raccoons.

FACTS: About wolves, foxes, and jackals

- **Big dogs**
  The dog family is a group of 35 species, including wolves, foxes, wild dogs, domestic dogs, jackals, and coyotes. All dogs have long legs, long narrow muzzles, and pointy canine teeth for eating flesh. They all also have a very good sense of smell.

- **Wolf packs**
  To hunt animals bigger than themselves, such as moose, deer, caribou, or musk oxen, wolves hunt together in packs. Wolf packs use smell to trace their prey, then try to isolate a weak animal within the herd and run it down.

- **Top dog**
  The eldest male and female in a pack maintain a strict hierarchy. Any wolf that tries to challenge their dominance is subdued or even expelled from the pack altogether. A pack may consist of 7–20 wolves.

The red fox is very adaptable and is often found living in cities, surviving by raiding disposal areas.

Foxes are clever hunters that prowl at night, alone or in pairs. They catch and eat rats, mice, and rabbits, but they will also willingly eat whatever is available, such as fruit, birds, and even human food scraps.

- **Jackal**
  Jackals live in Africa and Asia and look like small wolves. They hunt alone, not in packs, killing rats, mice, and birds. They only meet up when there is a chance of getting in on the leftovers from the kill of a lion or a leopard—their deadliest enemy.

Wolves once lived all over Europe and North America, but they have now been all but exterminated in Europe and live only in remote areas of North America.

FACTS: About bears

- **Where bears live**
  Bears live mostly in the northern hemisphere, in all kinds of environments. Only the spectacled bear lives in South America.

- **Brown bears**
  Brown bears are called "grizzly" because of the white furs on their shoulders.

- **Polar bears**
  White polar bears live in the Arctic and are the only bears that live on meat alone.

▲ *Brown bears, such as this Himalayan bear, hibernate. They put on weight during the fall and then retreat to a den for winter.*

▼ *The giant panda is one of the rarest animals, living only in the mountainous forests of central China, where its food, a certain kind of bamboo, grows. The bamboo is not very nutritious, so pandas spend 10–12 hours a day eating. They rarely have cubs, so the birth of a panda is precious.*

Pandas have a pad on their forepaws, called a sixth finger, to help them grip bamboo shoots as they chew

DATA: Pandas, bears and dogs

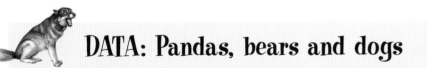

- **THE BIGGEST BEAR**
  The largest bear is the Kodiak, a type of brown bear from Alaska, which measures up to 8 feet and weighs up to 1,700 pounds.

- **THE LITTLEST BEAR**
  The smallest of the bears is the sun bear of the Southeast Asian rainforests. It is only about 56 inches tall and 60 pounds in weight.

- **WOLF RANGE**
  One wolf pack may inhabit a huge territory–up to 385 square miles.. They also cover great distances when hunting for food.

- **PANDA FOOD**
  Because bamboo has such a low nutritional value, pandas may eat up to 30 pounds of stems and leaves in a single day.

Sea mammals

MAMMALS ARE WARM-BLOODED CREATURES that breathe air and nurse their young on milk. Most are land animals, but they are remarkably adaptable and a few kinds spend all their lives in the sea, swimming around with the ease of a fish and only coming up for air occasionally. There are two main kinds of sea mammal. There are seals, sea lions, walruses, and sea cows, which mostly live in cold places and have both fur and a thick layer of fat called blubber to keep them warm. Then there are whales, dolphins, and porpoises, which have no fur, only blubber.

FACTS: About whales, dolphins, and porpoises

- **Cetaceans**
  Whales, dolphins, and porpoises are together known as cetaceans. Many are very gentle and intelligent creatures.

- **Breathing**
  Whales can stay hours underwater, but must eventually come up for air and spout out water from a blow hole on top.

- **Schools**
  Dolphins live in groups called schools up to 300 strong.

- **Dolphin talk**
  Dolphins keep in touch by clicks, barks, chattering sounds, screams, and moans, each of which seem to have a meaning that scientists do not understand. They find their way with sounds too high for the human ear to hear.

- **Whale sound**
  Whales "talk" with booming sounds. Finback whales can hear each other 500 miles apart.

Playful leaps, somersaults, and spins help knit groups of dolphins together

▲ Dolphins are very friendly, playful, and intelligent creatures. They form strong social relationships, with close mother-child bonds. Mating pairs seem to stay together for life.

- **Toothed and toothless whales**
  Some whales, such as the sperm and killer whales, have teeth and eat large fish. Others, such as the humpback and blue whales have no teeth. Instead, they have special comblike sieves in their mouths called baleens. They feed by straining tiny, shrimplike creatures called krill through the baleen.

FACTS: About seals, sea lions, and walruses

- **Going ashore**
  Seals, sea lions, and walruses are agile swimmers, but unlike whales and dolphins, they can live on land—although once ashore, they tend to waddle.

- **Breeding grounds**
  In spring and summer, thousands of seals crowd together on the shore to breed in vast colonies.

- **Seals and sea lions**
  Seals and sea lions look similar, but while seals have only ear openings, sea lions have ear flaps like most land mammals. Sea lions can also move their back flippers under their body to help them move around on land, unlike seals.

- **Seal meals**
  Seals and sea lions feed mainly on fish, but also eat shellfish. Crabeater seals feed mainly on krill, while bearded seals eat mainly clams.

- **Walruses**
  Walruses are big creatures a little like overgrown seals, growing up to 10 feet long, but they have massive tusks and face whiskers.

- **Leopard**
  The most ferocious seal is the Antarctic leopard, which grows to 13 feet and feeds on penguins.

▼ *Seals spend most of their lives in the sea, but come ashore to give birth. They stay on land for several weeks in colonies called rookeries, feeding their young milk. Every now and then, hunters will cull (kill) the young pups while they are still ashore—both for their fur and to keep down numbers. Many believe this is cruel. Others say it is necessary.*

▶ *Sea cows—dugongs and manatees—are plant-eating seals that live in warm coastal waters. Dugongs live around Africa and Asia. Manatees live in coastal rivers in the southeast USA, the West Indies, and northern South America. They greet one another with muzzle to muzzle kisses.*

Manatee

57

Pets

PEOPLE HAVE KEPT ANIMALS for many thousands of years—sometimes to help with particular tasks, sometimes as companions, sometimes simply to look at and admire. Dogs were first tamed more than 12,000 years ago to help with hunting, and since then many other animals have been adopted as pets—cats, birds, hamsters, guinea pigs, horses, and many others. There are more pet owners now than ever before, with millions of animals living in people's homes around the world. There are 500 million cats alone.

FACTS: About cats

- **Egyptian cats**
  The Ancient Egyptians tamed wild African bushcats to catch mice 3,500 years ago. Later, the Egyptians thought cats sacred.

- **Rough tongues**
  Cats' tongues are covered in bristles, which help them to lap up liquids and foods and to groom themselves, as with a comb.

- **Catnaps**
  Cats spend a lot of time sleeping—in short naps. But they can be awake and ready for action in an instant.

- **Cat litter**
  Most female cats are ready to be mothers by 10 months old—although many are neutered by their owners to stop them breeding. Female cats are pregnant for 9 weeks and give birth to a litter of 2–5 kittens.

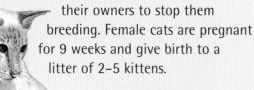

◀ There are many different breeds of cat, from common tabbies and tortoiseshells to valuable pedigree Siamese and Persian cats.

Dogs

There are more than 130 different breeds of domestic dog, but all are descended from the wolf, and, although tame, they retain many wolflike traits—body language, guarding territory, hiding bones, and so on.

▲ Many pets were originally working dogs, like the collie. Originally from Scotland, collies make wonderful sheepdogs. They are fast runners, quick learners and have an amazing sense of smell. They can even locate a sheep lost in the snow.

▶ Some pets were originally hunting dogs, such as terriers. Great diggers, with strong teeth and jaws, terriers were once used to dig out rats, rabbits, and badgers from the ground, and their name comes from the Latin terra, for earth.

▲ *Hamsters only live for two or three years. Golden hamsters (above)—the small variety kept as pets—all descend from a single wild litter found in Syria in 1930.*

▲ *Many pet dogs come from hunters and gun dogs, such as setters, pointers, and retrievers. When a red setter (above) spots a game bird, it crouches slightly and freezes, pointing its nose to the bird for the hunter.*

▽ *St. Bernards are one of many dogs used to help in emergencies and were once trained at the monastery of the Great St. Bernard Pass in Switzerland to rescue people who got lost in the surrounding mountains.*

FACTS: About fish

- **Tropical fish**
  Small tropical fish such as butterfly fish, angel fish, and guppies, are kept for their bright colors. But they are used to warm water, so must be kept in heated tanks.

- **Deadly fish**
  Some people like to keep piranhas from the Amazon. They have sharp teeth and are voracious flesh eaters, able to attack in a mass and eat large animals.

▶ *Descended from dull colored carp, goldfish were carefully bred by the Chinese and Japanese and are now the most popular of all pet fish.*

DATA: Pets

- **BIGGEST DOG**
  The tallest dog of all is the Irish wolfhound–44 inches to the shoulder.

- **HEAVIEST DOG**
  The heaviest dog is the St. Bernard–200 pounds.

- **SMALLEST DOG**
  The smallest dog is the Chihuahua–$5\frac{1}{2}$ inches tall.

- **OLD CAT**
  Cats may live up to the age of 20.

- **TINY FISH**
  The smallest pet fish are dwarf gobies, which can be less than $\frac{1}{2}$ an inch long.

Farm animals

BACON, HAMBURGERS, SHOES, BUTTER, woolen sweaters, milk, and many other things are provided by animals kept on farms-including cattle, sheep, pigs, and hens. All these animals are descended from wild animals, but they were domesticated-made tame-many thousands of years ago to give us a steady supply of meat, milk, eggs, fur, wool, and leather. Since then, farmers have created many hundreds of breeds of each animal, such as Herefordshire cows and Merino sheep, to create a more meaty animal, or one that gives better milk or wool.

FACTS: About cows

• **What are cows?**
Cows or cattle are descended from the wild auroch tamed 9,000 years ago. Male cattle are bulls; females cows; and young cattle calves.

• **Dairy cow**
Females are kept for milk, butter, and cheese and called dairy cows. They give birth to a calf each year and after the birth provide milk twice a day for 10 months.

• **Beef breeds**
Male cattle are raised for meat. Cattle also provide leather and glue and droppings for fertilizer. Beef breeds are rounder and heftier than dairy cows.

• **Chewing the cud**
Cows chew the cud. They have four stomachs and after swallowing food they bring it back up into their mouths for further chewing.

▲ *Goats are kept for meat, milk, skins, and wool. Goats' milk is very good for people who are allergic to richer cows' milk, while Angora and Kashmir goats provide very fine wool. Goats are often kept in rocky mountain areas because they are agile and have strong enough jaws and stomachs to live off coarse vegetation.*

▼ *Pigs are kept for meat—pork, bacon, and ham—and leather. Their hairs are also used to make artists' brushes. The European domestic pig is descended from the European wild boar, which is much hairier and darker than the domestic pig, and also has tusks. Most pigs are now raised on factory farms where they are fed on special diets that help them grow rapidly.*

FACTS: About poultry

On a few farms, hens may scratch around for insects and seeds in the farmyard and lay their eggs in a small hut called a coop. These are called free-range hens.

- **Fowl**
Ducks, geese, turkeys, and chickens are all called poultry, and are bred in captivity to be eaten or to provide eggs, meat, and feathers.

- **Old hens**
Chickens have been domesticated since the 5th century BC and there are over 100 different varieties. Females are called hens; males are called roosters or cocks.

Turkeys are a type of pheasant. There are several different species, but they all descend from the native wild turkey of North America.

- **Egg laying**
Hens lay one or two eggs a day. To keep them laying, the eggs must be taken everyday. If not, the hens wait until they have a small collection, then sit on them, keeping them warm for about 20 days until chicks hatch.

- **Battery hens**
Very few hens are free range. In Europe and North America, most are crowded into rows of small boxes called batteries inside a heated building, where they are fed and watered, and waste and eggs are collected automatically.

- **Turkey tail**
Male turkeys have 14–18 feathers in their tails, and when courting females, they spread these feathers out and raise them above their backs. All species of turkey have a "wattle" of bare, floppy skin that hangs down from their head and neck.

- **Turkish turkeys**
The name turkey may have come from the mistaken idea that the bird came from Turkey.

DATA: Farm animals

- **COW BREED**
There are 200 or so different types of domestic cow.

- **HEAD OF SHEEP**
There are more than 680 million sheep in the world and 800 different breeds.

- **MILK PRODUCTION**
Cows produce around 4.5 gallons of milk a day, or 1,660 gallons a year.

- **TURKEY EGGS**
Turkey hens lay only about 12 eggs a year.

The sheep was one of the first animals to be domesticated, some 10,000 years ago. Wooly sheep such as the Merino have fine wool suitable for clothing or coarse hair for carpets. Hairy sheep are bred for milk and meat. Australia, New Zealand, and South America have the right climate and the right pastures for sheep rearing, and there are vast sheep farms or "stations" here.

Tropical birds

THE TROPICS ARE HOME TO some of the world's most beautiful and spectacular birds. In the rain forests in particular there is a huge variety of colorful birds, because color is a real asset in finding a mate. In Indonesia and Australia, there are birds of paradise and lyre birds with magnificent tail feathers. In South America, there are the brilliantly colored cotingas and huge-beaked toucans. Then there are parrots, such as macaws and budgerigars, and big birds, such as flamingoes and hornbills, and tiny birds, such as hummingbirds.

FACTS: About weaver birds

- **Home makers**
Weaver birds are small birds that live in the tropics of Africa and Asia. They get their name because many weave elaborate nests.

- **Nest weaving**
Using their bills and feet they make pouch-shaped nests from plant fibers, which they suspend from tree branches, away from predators. The entrance is usually a funnel with a hole at the end, just big enough for the weaver but small enough to keep other unfriendly animals out.

- **The biggest bird nests**
Sociable weaver birds of South Africa build big nests containing enough separate cavities for hundreds of pairs of birds under one communal roof. Each has its own entrance tunnel, complete with grass stems pointing downward over it to help keep enemies out.

▶ The nest of the village weaver is begun by the male bird. When he has found a female willing to move in, she finishes off inside. The male then leaves her to lay her eggs while he goes off to start another nest.

▲ Pelicans are fish-eating birds with special pouched bills which they use to scoop up fish from the water. Their pouches can hold as much as two or three times as their stomachs.

▶ Like all bee-eaters, the carmine bee-eater has a long tail—the streamers are up to 5 inches. Their long, downward-pointing, curved bills are perfect for catching bees on the wing. They rub the bee against a branch to remove the sting. Carmine bee-eaters of Africa often ride on the backs of other birds, such as ostriches and storks, as well as grazing mammals, such as antelopes and cattle, in order to pick up insects disturbed by their feet.

▶ *The Paradise whydah lives in Africa, and the male has perhaps the most spectacular tail feathers of any bird, four times as long as its body. When in flight, the whydah holds two short upper tail feathers upright while the longer ones dangle down. To attract females, it flies above her so that the long feathers wave up and down in an attractive way!*

The tail feathers of a breeding male can be as long as 11 inches

◀ *The hoatzin is a large ungainly bird that lives in the forests of northern South America. It is an awkward flier so tends to glide from tree to tree. The young have two hooked claws on their wings to help them move around.*

DATA: Tropical birds

- **BIGGEST NEST**
  A South African sociable weaver bird nest can be up to 13 feet deep and 24 ½ feet long.

- **OLDEST BIRD**
  The longest living captive birds are the sulphur crested cockatoos of Australia–up to 80 years.

FACTS: About parrots and cockatoos

- **Bill for nuts**
  Parrots are colorful birds of the tropics with curved bills for eating fruit and seeds and cracking nuts.

- **Parrot feet**
  Parrot feet have two toes pointing forward and two backward, allowing them to grip onto branches and hold food.

- **Three species**
  There are three groups of parrots—true parrots, cockatoos, and lories—making 330 different species altogether. The largest is the hyacinth macaw (40 inches bill to tail). The smallest is the tiny buff-faced pygmy parrot 3 ½ inches (8.4cm).

- **Mimic**
  Some parrots, such as the African gray parrot, can imitate the human voice.

▲ *Like all parrots the scarlet macaw can be incredibly noisy, with a raucous, rasping caw.*

◀ *Male Andean cock-of-the-rocks are famous for their color and their spectacular courtship routines.*

Temperate birds

BIRDS IN TEMPERATE REGIONS may not be as colorful and spectacular as those of the tropics, but there is an enormous range and variety. There are town and garden birds, such as the sparrow, the bluejay, and the pigeon. There are woodland birds, such as the wood pigeon and the nightjar. There are birds that live near water too-freshwater birds, such as ducks and swans, waders, such as curlews and redshanks, and seabirds, such as gulls and puffins. Then there are the magnificent birds of prey, such as eagles, kestrels, hawks, and falcons, and the night-hunting owls.

FACTS: About water birds

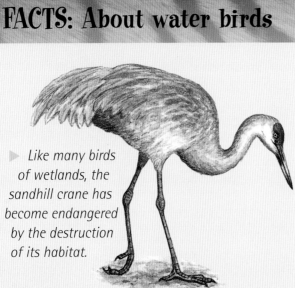

▷ Like many birds of wetlands, the sandhill crane has become endangered by the destruction of its habitat.

- **Waders**
  Wading birds, such as curlews and plovers, have long legs for wading through the water and long bills for probing around in the mud to look for food.

- **Waterfowl**
  Waterfowl, such as ducks, geese, and swans, have webbed feet for swimming and long bendy necks for reaching into the water.

- **Seabirds**
  Many seabirds are very good divers and roam the open sea looking for food. They often lay their eggs in nesting grounds high up on the cliffs so that they are kept safely out of the reach of predators.

▷ Like many birds, the redstart feeds on insects, and has a wide beak for catching them in flight. It was originally a woodland bird, but has adapted well to environmental changes.

◁ The waxwing gets its name from the waxy red tips on some of its wing feathers. Like many seed and fruit-eating birds, it has a short pincer like beak for cracking seeds.

▲ Common pheasants came originally from Asia, like this Monal pheasant. But they have adapted well to other areas and are now the most widespread of all game birds.

DATA: Temperate birds

- **ANCIENT BIRD**
  The oldest known bird was a Cockatoo of London Zoo, that died in 1982, aged 80.

- **SHARPEST EYES**
  The keen-eyed peregrine falcon can spot a pigeon at 5 miles away.

▲ *Jays are seed-eating birds that like acorns, which they bury for winter food. But they sometimes steal nestlings and eggs from the nests of other birds.*

▼ *The pigeons that swarm over many city squares are all descended from domestic pigeons, which came in turn from the wild rock dove. They are called "feral" because they were once tame and are now wild.*

FACTS: About birds of prey

▶ *The peregrine falcon can plummet at speeds of 110 mph when diving down on prey.*

- **What are birds of prey?**
  Birds of prey are hunting birds that feed on small animals, such as birds and rabbits. All have sharp, hooked bills, strong feet with talons, and very good eyesight and hearing.

- **Different quarry**
  Different birds specialize in hunting different things: honey buzzards eat bees and have talons shaped for digging out nests; eagles have large talons for snatching up rabbits and squirrels; harriers eat snakes and other reptiles; ospreys specialize in catching fish, such as salmon.

- **Birds under threat**
  Many birds of prey have been endangered by hunting, egg collecting, and gamekeepers who want to stop the birds of prey killing game birds and pigeons.

▶ *Owls hunt at night and have large, round eyes to see well in poor light, but their hearing is also so sharp they can catch prey in pitch dark by sound alone.*

Reptiles

REPTILES ARE SCALY-SKINNED CREATURES such as crocodiles, lizards, and snakes. They are sometimes said to be cold-blooded. But their blood is not cold; it can be as warm as a mammal's. Mammals get their warmth by eating. Reptiles can survive on very little food, but they depend on the sun for warmth and must continually shuttle between warm and cold places to stay at the right temperature. They may spend hours basking in the sun, gaining enough energy to go hunting for food. But they depend on the sun for warmth, so they cannot live in cold places.

FACTS: About snakes

- **What are snakes?**
Snakes are thin, limbless reptiles that live mostly in warm regions. They are predators, but with no limbs; they kill their prey with poison or by constricting (squeezing) them to death.

- **Tongue scent**
Snakes have no ears, but sense their prey from sound vibrations on the ground. They also use their tongues to smell with—but only use their eyes when close to as their eyesight is poor.

- **Snakes with bite**
Many snakes are venomous—that is, they have a poisonous bite. Those with fangs in the front of their mouths, such as vipers and rattlesnakes, are more dangerous than back-fanged snakes—because back-fanged snakes must get a victim fully into their mouths to bite.

- **Big squeeze**
Boas and pythons kill large victims by constriction. The snake coils itself around its victim. Each time the trapped animal breathes out the snake tightens its hold until its prey finally suffocates.

The taipan is a large, poisonous snake from Australia that grows up to 10 feet—large for a poisonous snake. It is from the same family as the cobra—the elapids—all of which have venom in their front fangs.

Like all vipers, the Gaboon viper has long fangs in the front of its mouth, which hinge back into the mouth when not in use. The fangs are hollow and act as "syringes"—injecting venom straight into the victim when the snake bites.

Geckos can climb up straight walls and even run across ceilings because they have feet like suction caps. Their toes are flat with pads underneath them and these pads are covered with hundreds of tiny hooks, which can grip onto flat surfaces.

FACTS: About alligators

- **Crocodiles vs. alligators**
Crocodiles and alligators are large reptiles that live in warm rivers and swamps. Crocodiles have thinner snouts and a fourth tooth on the lower jaw, which is visible when the mouth is shut.

- **Floating predators**
Alligators and crocodiles are predators that lurk under the surface with just their eyes and nostrils above the water and can take prey by surprise by springing out suddenly.

The alligator of the Florida Everglade swamps is now a protected animal because it was once endangered by hunters wanting its skin.

Turtles and tortoises are together known as chelonians, and all live inside an armored shell of bony plates. On their back is a domed "carapace," underneath is a flat "plastron." Some can pull their arms, legs, and head right in. They are slow moving, but withdrawing inside their shell protects them.

The frilled-necked lizard of Australia may not be very big, but it makes up for its lack of size with its enormous frill. Normally, the frill hangs limp, but it spreads out up to 10 inches whenever the lizard is threatened, making it look three times as large and twice as dangerous.

Iguanas, such as the Madagascan iguana (below), are large, tropical lizards. The marine iguanas of the Galapagos are one of the very few lizards that live in the sea. They can stay under the water for up to an hour.

Amphibians

AMPHIBIANS ARE CREATURES, such as frogs, toads, newts, and salamanders, that live part of their lives on land and part in the water. Most begin life by hatching in water from big clusters of eggs called spawn. At this stage, they are more like fish. But they soon grow legs and develop lungs for breathing air. Before long they are ready to clamber ashore, where most will spend their adult lives. Even so, they rarely stray far from water. They return to water to lay their eggs because their eggs, unlike those of reptiles, are not waterproof and so would dry out in air.

FACTS: About frogs and toads

- **Skin breathers**
  Most frogs breathe partly through their skin and so need to keep damp all the time. They are very good swimmers and, except for tree frogs, spend most of their time in or near water.

- **High jumpers**
  Neither frogs nor toads have tails as adults, but they have long, strong back legs for jumping.

- **Biggest frog**
  The largest frog is the goliath from West Africa which measures up to 32 inches when stretched out and weighs up to 6 pounds. The smallest is a Brazilian frog—$\frac{1}{3}$ inch.

▲ *Tree frogs of tropical rainforests take advantage of other moisture sources to live in the trees far from water.*

- **Flying frog**
  Flying frogs are tree frogs that can glide through the air. They have sticky disks on their fingers for gripping onto branches and their hands and feet are webbed to act as airbrakes.

- **Warty toad**
  Generally, toads have drier, wartier skin than frogs and have shorter hind legs, which are better for walking than jumping, unlike a frog's. Toads are also less active than frogs.

▲ *Poison arrow frogs of the Amazon are brightly colored to warn that their sweat glands contain a deadly poison—which the Indians used to smear on their arrows.*

- **Baby swallower**
  The male Darwin's frog of Chile swallows the spawn left by the female and keeps it in his throat until it hatches as little tadpoles.

FACTS: About newts and salamanders

- **Lizard lookalikes**
Newts and salamanders look a little like lizards, but they are amphibians, not reptiles like lizards, and begin life in water. Newts live in temperate climates and hibernate during the winter under logs and stones. Salamanders live in warmer areas and so do not need to hibernate.

- **Giant salamander**
The giant salamander grows up to 6 feet long.

- **Colored newts**
Many male newts have bright colors and special markings during their mating season to attract females. The crested newt has a bright orange or yellow belly, as well as a bumpy crest down the length of its back.

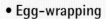

Newts are the most water-loving of all the amphibians, spending much of their lives in ponds.

- **Egg-wrapping**
To protect their eggs from predators, female newts wrap each egg in a leaf with their feet.

- **Fire salamander**
Fire salamanders got their name because they shelter underneath logs and so when in the past logs were burned on fires, salamanders hiding underneath would come rushing out of the fire.

1. The fertilized eggs of a frog are called spawn. Each of the blobs in spawn is an egg containing an embryo, protected in a bag of jelly

2. The eggs hatch in water after a week or so into fishlike tadpoles, which swim around, breathe through gills, and grow rapidly

3. After 7 weeks, the tadpole begins to grow hind legs, then front legs. Soon the young froglet begins to breathe through lungs rather than gills

As they grow from eggs to adults, all amphibians, such as the frog, go through a series of dramatic changes, called a metamorphosis. Each creature has its own special way of developing. But the sequence shown here for the frog is fairly typical.

4. The froglet's legs go on growing and its tail shortens. After 14 weeks, the frog is an adult and leaves the water

Insects

INSECTS MAY BE TINY but they are by far the most numerous of all creatures. There are more than a million known species, and they are found almost everywhere. Ants scurry along the ground. Bees buzz around hives. Butterflies flutter over flowers. Insects are very varied in look, but all have six legs and a body divided into three sections—head, thorax, and abdomen. They also have two compound eyes with anything from six to 30,000 lenses and a variety of other sensors, such as antennae (feelers), which they can use to hear, taste, and smell.

FACTS: About butterflies, moths, and caterpillars

• **Butterflies and moths**
Butterflies and moths are both part of a big group of insects called Lepidoptera, which means "scaly wings," because their wings are covered in tiny dustlike scales.

• **What's the difference?**
Butterflies are usually brightly colored and fly during the day. They have thin, hairless bodies and a pair of clubbed antennae. Moths tend to be drabber, because they rest during the day—on trees and dead leaves—and so must be camouflaged. They have plump, hairy bodies and straight antennae.

• **Caterpillars**
Butterflies and moths begin life as an egg, then hatch as long thin caterpillars, which eat leaves voraciously for a month.

Butterflies such as the red admiral can migrate astonishing distances, as far as many birds— even crossing oceans, with the help of the wind.

• **Chrysalis and cocoon**
When the caterpillar is ready, it spins a cocoon of silk around itself or creates a hard shell called a chrysalis. Inside, it becomes a pupa, grows wings and, amazingly, changes to an adult butterfly before emerging.

• **Nectar seeker**
Most butterflies feed, if at all, only on nectar, the sweet juice of flowers, and so spend their brief lives fluttering from bloom to bloom.

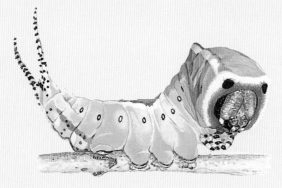

Caterpillars are fat and slow-moving, so are very vulnerable to predators. But the Puss Moth caterpillar can scare smaller enemies by rearing up, waving its tail and squirting formic acid.

The head consists of mouth parts, eyes, and antennae

The thorax is packed with muscles that move the legs as well as the main body organs

Insects breathe through holes in their sides called spiracles

The abdomen holds all the insect's digestive organs and its sex organs

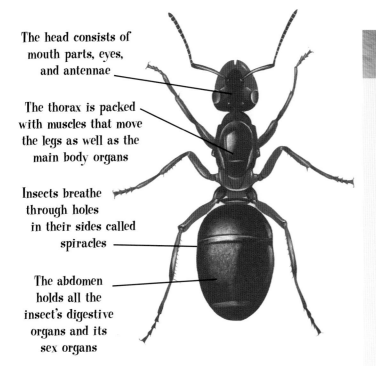

Insects look very different from other animals. Not only are their bodies split into three sections, but they have no bones. Instead, they have a rigid shell or "exoskeleton," made of a tough substance called chitin.

FACTS: About bees

- **Beehive**
  Bees live together in large numbers in hives or nests. In each colony, there is one queen, many female workers, and a few drones (males).

- **Queen bee**
  Only the queen can lay eggs—up to 1,000 a day. Drones exist only to mate with the queen, after which they die.

- **Worker bee**
  Workers collect pollen and nectar from flowers and bring it to the nest. Pollen is fed to grubs and nectar is used for honey.

A honeybee's main protection is the sting in its tail. Its bright yellow and black stripes are a warning.

Termites are insects that live in huge colonies in the tropics. Together, they build huge mounds to live in out of dust and saliva, complete with air conditioning. Some termite mounds can be 30 feet tall.

Dragonflies are large, fast-flying insects that can dart at up to 35 mph. Their four wings move independently of one another and make a rattling sound. They can also fly backward.

DATA: Insects

- **LONGEST INSECT**
  The world's longest insect is the giant stick insect of Borneo, which grows up to 13 inches long.

- **SMALLEST INSECT**
  The fairy fly is just $1\frac{1}{125}$ inches long.

- **AN ANT'S STRENGTH**
  An ant can lift 50 times its own weight–that is like you lifting a truck!

Key facts: Animals

Kingdoms

1. Monerans
Simple single-cell organisms with no nucleus, e.g. bacteria.
2. Protista
Mostly single-cell organisms with a nucleus, e.g. amebas.
3. Fungi
Multicelled organisms that feed on living or dead organic matter, e.g. molds.
4. Plantae
Multicelled organisms, such as trees, plants, and grasses.
5. Animalia
Animals—multicelled organisms that must find food and can move around.

The animal kingdom:
- **Vertebrates**
  Mammals
  Birds
  Amphibians
  Reptiles
  Jawless fish
  Sea squirts
  Sharks and rays
  Bony fish
- **Invertebrates**
  Echinoderms
  Arthropods
  Velvetworms, lampshells etc.
  Worms of all kinds
  Sponges
  Cnidaria
  Mollusks

Animal classification

Classification of a lion:

Kingdom
Animalia
Multicelled organisms that cannot make their own food.
Phylum
Chordate
Animals that have a single nerve cord at some stage during their life.
Class
Mammal
Animals that suckle their young on milk and have hair or fur.
Order
Carnivore
Land mammals adapted to hunting.

Family
Cats
Have sharp, retractable front claws.
Genus
Big cats
Includes five species—lions, tigers, leopards, snow leopards, and jaguars.
Species
Lion

Males, females, and babies

Animal	Male	Female	Young
Antelope	Buck	Doe	Kid
Bobcat	Tom	Lioness	Kitten
Buffalo	Bull	Cow	Calf
Camel	Bull	Cow	Calf
Caribou	Stag	Doe	Fawn
Duck	Drake	Duck	Duckling
Fish	Cock	Hen	Fry
Goat	Billygoat	Nannygoat	Kid
Goose	Gander	Goose	Gosling
Seal	Bull	Cow	Pup
Swan	Cob	Pen	Cygnet
Weasel	Boar	Cow	Kit

Animal habitats

Freshwater lakes
- otter, water vole, harvest mouse
- reed warbler, heron, kingfisher, marsh harrier, coot
- frogs, toads, newts
- dragonfly, pondskater, waterboatman, mayfly
- stickleback, trench, pike, perch

Tundra and Arctic
- polar bear, Arctic fox, Arctic hare, gray wolf, vole, ermine, lemming, musk ox, caribou
- eagles, grouse, plover, goose, snowy owl
- mosquito

Mountains
- ibex, chamois deer, yak, llama, vicuna, puma, snow leopard, lynx, chinchilla, marmot
- eagles, condor, lammergeier
- ice worm

Tropical grasslands
- giraffe, zebra, antelope, lion, leopard, cheetah, elephant, water buffalo, mongoose, hyena, jackal
- ostrich, marabou stork, oxpecker, weaver bird, secretary bird, vulture
- Eastern brown snakes, red-bellied snakes
- dung beetle, termite, locust

Temperate grasslands
- saiga antelope, pronghorn antelope, bison, prairie dog, mole rat, coyote, fox
- rhea, guanaco, buzzard
- grass snakes, lizards
- grasshoppers, flies

Tropical forests
- monkeys, leopard, shrew, sloth, coati, opossum, okapi, tamandua, jaguar
- macaws, parrots, toucans, hummingbirds, jacamars
- viper, anaconda, python, tree frogs, iguana, crocodiles, turtles
- morpho butterfly, hunting spider, ants

Temperate forests
- squirrel, skunk, badger, mouse, raccoon, hedgehog, chipmunk, beaver, rabbit, fox, deer, bear, wolf, wild boar
- warbler, tits, woodpeckers, woodcock, jay, owl
- salamanders, slugs
- ants, purple emperor butterfly, moths, beetles, earthworm, snails, centipede

Deserts
- camels, addax, fennec fox, long-eared jackrabbit, kangaroo rat, gundi, jerboa
- roadrunner, hummingbird, vultures, nighthawk, burrowing owl, sand grouse
- spiny lizard, gila monster, rattlesnake, gecko, thorny devil, toroises
- scorpion, antlion, spiders

Seashore
- anenomes, barnacles, mussels, starfish, crabs, sea cucumber, cockles, lugworm, sea urchin, scallop, limpets,
- gulls, tern, gannet, pelican

Oceans
- Surface waters: seal, porpoise, shark, mackerel, jellyfish, turtle, seahorse
- Midocean: squid, octopus, swordfish, hatchet fish, lanternfish, flatfish
- Deep sea: ray, gulper eel, angler fish, giant squid, sperm whale

Key facts: Animals

Birds

- **The biggest bird**
  The biggest bird is the ostrich, which can grow up to 9 feet tall.
- **The smallest bird**
  The smallest bird is the bee hummingbird, which is just $2\frac{1}{5}$ inches long.
- **The biggest flying bird**
  The biggest flying bird is the Mute swan which can weigh up to 49 pounds.
- **The biggest bird of prey**
  The Andean condor can weigh 24 pounds or more.
- **The fastest flier**
  The fastest flier is the peregrine falcon, which can dive up to 210 mph.
- **The oldest bird**
  Cocky the cockatoo of London Zoo was more than 80 when he died in 1982.
- **The longest journey**
  A Common tern flew 13,970 miles from Russia down through the Atlantic over Africa and the Indian Ocean to Australia.
- **The most time in the air**
  No bird spends more time flying than the sooty tern, which can remain in the air for 3–10 years.
- **The biggest egg**
  The biggest egg is the ostrich, which can grow up to 8 inches across.
- **The highest flier**
  The highest flight was by a Ruppell's vulture, which hit a plane at 36,989 feet.
- **The fastest swimmer**
  A gentoo penguin gets to 17 mph.

Sea creatures

- **The smallest fish**
  The smallest fish is the Indo-Pacific dwarf, which is only $\frac{3}{5}$ inch long.
- **The largest fish**
  The largest fish is the whale shark, which can grow more than 40 feet long.
- **The fastest fish**
  The fastest fish is the sailfish, which can travel at up to 68 mph.
- **The oldest fish**
  The Whale shark can live to more than 70 years.
- **The deadliest jellyfish**
  The deadly Australian Sea Wasp can kill a man in just one minute.
- **The noisiest animal**
  The noisiest animal is the Blue whale. Its sounds can be detected from 500 miles away.
- **The smallest crab**
  The smallest crab is the pea crab, which really is as small as a pea.
- **The largest turtle**
  The largest turtle is the Pacific leatherback, which grows up to 7 feet long.
- **The longest journey**
  European eels travel 4,650 miles on their spawning migration from the Baltic to the Sargasso Sea.

Mammals

- **The biggest mammal**
  The biggest mammal is the Blue whale, which can grow up to 110 feet long and weigh up to 210 tons.
- **The biggest land mammal**
  The biggest land mammal is the African bush elephant, which can grow up 13 feet tall and weigh up to 13 tons.
- **The tallest mammal**
  The tallest mammal is the giraffe, which can grow more than 20 feet tall.
- **The smallest mammal**
  The smallest mammal is the bumblebee bat of Thailand, which weighs less than $\frac{1}{10}$ ounce.
- **The smallest land mammal**
  The smallest land mammal is the Sari's pygmy, which is less than 2 inches long.
- **The fastest sprinting land mammal**
  The fastest land mammal is the cheetah, which can reach 60 mph for short bursts.
- **The fastest running land mammal**
  The fastest running land mammal over a sustained distance is the North American pronghorn antelope, which can keep up 35 mph for more than 4 miles.
- **The fastest marine mammal**
  The fastest swimming mammal is the killer whale, which can reach 35 mph.
- **The highest jumper**
  The highest jumping animals are pumas and leopards, which can jump more than 16 feet.
- **The oldest mammal**
  The oldest mammal (apart from humans, of course) is the elephant, which can live more than 70 years.

Reptiles

- **The largest reptile**
  The largest reptile is the estuarine crocodile of SE Asia, which can grow to more than 16 feet in length.
- **The biggest lizard**
  The biggest lizard is the komodo dragon which grows more than 10 feet and has been said to grow to 30 feet.
- **The biggest amphibian**
  The biggest amphibian is the Chinese giant salamander which is more than 3 feet long.
- **The longest snake**
  The longest snake may be the reticulated python at more than 30 feet long.
- **The most poisonous snake**
  The most poisonous snake is the Marine Cobra of the western Pacific.

Insects

- **The heaviest insects**
  The heaviest flying insects are the Goliath beetles of Africa, at up to $3\frac{3}{5}$ ounces.
- **The longest insect**
  The longest insects are stick insects, which can grow up to 16 inches long.
- **The fastest flier**
  The Australian dragonfly reaches 36 mph.
- **The largest butterfly**
  The Queen Alexandra's birdwing of Papua New Guinea can be up to 10 inches across.
- **The loudest insect**
  Male cicadas (like crickets) rub their abdomens so loud they can be heard at 1,300 feet.

Quiz: Animals

1. What is the world's smallest bird?

2. What is the smallest land mammal?

3. What's a beaver's home called?

4. What is a margay?

5. What bird makes the longest migration?

6. What sea mammals have two long tusks?

7. What do seals mainly eat?

8. What do whales have on the tops of their heads?

9. Which is the largest meat eater in the Arctic?

10. Which animal can sprint the fastest?

11. What is a group of lions called?

12. What is the world's biggest mammal?

13. What animal has a horn on the end of its snout?

14. How can you tell an adult male lion from a female?

15. Which is the biggest bird of prey?

16. What are the claws of a bird of prey called?

17. The sooty tern can fly non stop for 10 years: true or false?

18. Crocodiles, lizards, and snakes are all kinds of what?

19. The male Darwin's frog swallows the spawn laid by the female and keeps it in its throat until it hatches into little tadpoles: true or false?

20. Can a butterfly fly across an ocean?

Answers:

1. The bee hummingbird (at 2.¼ inches long)
2. Savi's pygmy shrew
3. A lodge
4. One of the smaller 'big cats'
5. Common Tern
6. Walrus
7. Mainly fish
8. A blowhole, for breathing out
9. The Polar bear
10. The cheetah, reaching speeds of up to 60 mph
11. A pride
12. The Blue whale
13. A rhinoceros
14. An adult male has a big mane; a lioness does not
15. The Andean condor
16. Talons
17. True
18. Reptiles
19. True
20. Yes

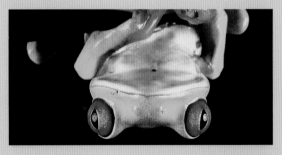

PLANTS

Plants

THERE ARE MORE THAN 250,000 different kinds of plant, ranging from tiny plankton barely visible under a microscope to giant trees hundreds of feet tall, the world's largest living things. They grow almost everywhere on land and in the sea, on plains and on mountaintops, even in deserts and snowy wastes. Indeed, 40 percent of the world's land is covered by trees and grass. What makes plants very different from animals is that they do not move around and have no need of senses (or a brain) because they can make their own food from sunlight.

FACTS: About stems

- **The plant stem**
  The stem supports the plant's flowers and leaves. It is also a pipe to take water, minerals, and food up and down between the roots and the leaves. Water goes up from the roots via tubes called xylem. Food goes down from the leaves in tubes called phloem.

- **Woody and herbaceous**
  Many plants have stems that are green and bendy. They are called herbaceous plants, because many are herbs, such as parsley. Woody plants, such as trees, have stiff stems or trunks covered in bark.

▶ *Bamboo is an unusual plant. It is a kind of grass and starts off with a soft, bendy, herbaceous stem. But as it grows, very rapidly, the stem becomes hard, tough, and woody.*

FACTS: About leaves

- **Sun traps**
  Leaves are a plant's solar cells and catch the light to make the food the plant needs to grow. Most are broad and flat to catch as much sun as possible.

- **Stalk and blade**
  Each leaf is attached to the stem by a small stalk called a petiole. The flat part of the leaf is called the blade.

- **Simple and compound**
  Some leaves, such as maple leaves, are called simple leaves because they only have one blade. Other leaves, such as those of the walnut and willow, are called compound because they have a number of blades on the same stalk.

- **Biggest leaves**
  The biggest leaves belong to the raffia palm tree, which can grow 65 feet long.

▶ *The lines on leaves are veins that not only provide a frame to support the leaf, but carry water in and the food the leaf makes out.*

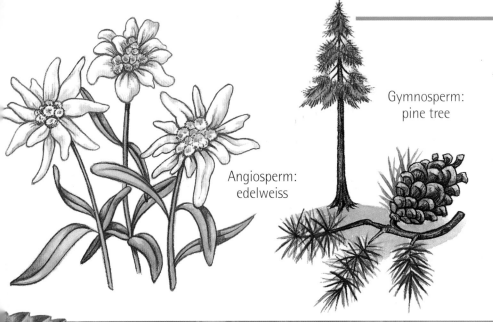

Angiosperm:
edelweiss

Gymnosperm:
pine tree

◄ *The first plants to grow on land were plants, such as fungi and lichen, which grow from tiny cells called spores. But most plants today grow not from spores but seeds. Unlike the more primitive spore-making plants, seed-making plants have stems, leaves, and often roots and flowers. Seed-making plants are divided into gymnosperms which have cones, and angiosperms, which bear flowers.*

FACTS: About photosynthesis

◄ *Leaves are made up from a lot of tiny parcels called cells. The wall is made of a tough material called cellulose. Inside are bundles, called chloroplasts, which are the plant's solar energy converters.*

When the sun shines, chlorophyll in the leaves soaks up the energy to split water into oxygen and hydrogen

Carbon dioxide is absorbed through pores in the leaves called stomata

In the leaves hydrogen joins with carbon dioxide to make sugar

The remaining oxygen goes out into the air. This is called respiration

Water and minerals are drawn up through the stem

- **Food making**
Plants make their food by absorbing sunlight in a process called photosynthesis. The sun gives the plant energy to change carbon dioxide from the air and hydrogen from water into food.

- **Green packages**
Photosynthesis occurs in tiny packages in leaf cells called chloroplasts. These contain a green substance called chlorophyll, which makes leaves green. It is this that soaks up the sun.

▶ *In photosynthesis, chlorophyll in the leaves uses the sun's energy to turn carbon dioxide from the air and hydrogen from water into sugars, which the plant uses as fuel for growth.*

Minerals are drawn from the soil

Water is drawn up through the roots

Roots and bulbs

THE GREEN AND COLORFUL PARTS of a plant are the leaves and flowers you see above the ground–but there is more to a plant beneath the surface. This is where the plant's roots are, growing down into soil or water. Roots not only hold the plant in place, anchoring it in the soil, but also draw up the water and minerals that the plant needs to grow. In some plants, such as beets, the roots also act as a food store. Sometimes, new plants can grow, or plants that die back can regrow, from the parts below ground, which form bulbs, corms, rhizomes, and tubers.

FACTS: About roots

▲ *Root vegetables are vegetables that grow underground. But not all of them are really roots. Carrots and beets are true roots, but potatoes are tubers, which are underground stems, and onions are bulbs, which are underground leaves.*

- **Growing plant**
  When a plant begins to grow, the seed sends out a single primary root. This quickly branches out into secondary roots. The tips of these are protected by a root cap as they probe out through the soil.

- **Taproots**
  Some plants have just one very large root, with only a few very fine roots sprouting off it. The large root is called a taproot.

- **Fibrous roots**
  Some plants, such as grasses, have a lot of fine roots spreading out in a dense mat. These are called fibrous roots. Some rye grasses grow 7,000 miles of roots in one chunk of soil.

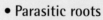

- **Root hairs**
  Every root has very fine "root hairs" branching off it. These hairs are very good at soaking up water and minerals from the soil.

- **Parasitic roots**
  Parasitic plants are unable to take up water and minerals from the soil themselves. Instead they draw their food from other plants. Mistletoe, for instance, wraps its roots around apple trees.

- **Climbing roots**
  Some climbing plants, such as ivy, don't only have roots underground, but on the stem, too. These stem roots serve mainly to hold the plant onto trees, walls, and fences.

- **Deepest roots**
  The roots of a wild fig tree in Transvaal, South Africa go down 400 feet into the ground. An elm tree seen growing in Largs, Scotland, had roots 360 feet deep.

FACTS: About bulbs, corms, rhizomes, and tubers

- **New from old**
  Some plants only grow once from a seed. But many perennials can die back, then grow anew again and again from parts of a root or stem. This is called vegetative propagation.

- **Rhizomes**
  Plants, such as irises, sprout from thick stems called rhizomes which grow sideways beneath the ground.

- **Tubers**
  Sometimes, the end of a rhizome swells into lumps called tubers. Potatoes are tubers.

- **Corms**
  Flowers, such as crocuses, grow from the bulbous base to their stem, called a corm.

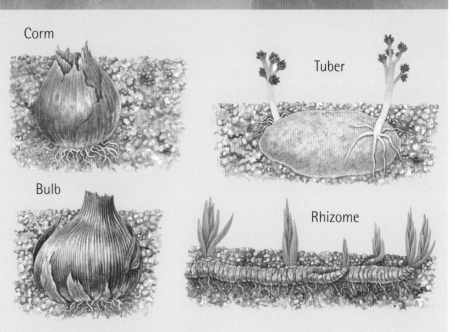

Corm

Tuber

Bulb

Rhizome

▲ To survive the winter, many plants die back to leave nothing visible above the ground. But the plant stays alive in the form of a corm, tuber, bulb, or rhizome. All of these are "storage organs," providing food to sustain the plant through the winter and to feed new shoots when they reemerge the following spring.

- **Bulbs**
  Bulbs, such as onions, look like corms, but they are actually made of leaf parts rather than the stem, which is why the onion has layers.

- **Food stores**
  Plants, such as lupins, grow in a ring around the outside of an old stem as the stem gets older and grows wider.

FACTS: About runners and suckers

◄ Strawberry plants are plants that spread by growing runners—that is, long stems that creep over the ground. Here and there along the stem it puts down new roots and a new plant grows.

Strawberry runners

- **Creeping stems**
  Some plants, such as roses, propagate (grow new plants) not from seeds or bulbs, corms, rhizomes, or tubers, but from long thin stems that creep over the ground (runners) or under it (suckers).

- **Buried leaves**
  With some plants, such as begonias, new plants can grow from broken leaves that get embedded in the soil.

Flowers, seeds & fruit

MOST OF THE WORLD'S PLANTS are flowers. Not only garden and wild flowers, but many trees and every herb, shrub, grain, fruit, and vegetable is a flowering plant, or "angiosperm." The blooms may not all be as big and beautiful as those of a rose, but all flowering plants have flowers, and all serve a purpose. Flowers are not just for show–they are sexual, just like us, and contain male parts that make the pollen to fertilize the eggs, or "ovules," made by female parts. Only when these come together can flowers create the fruit and seeds from which new plants will grow.

FACTS: About seeds and fruit

- **Seeds**
Seeds are the tiny packages from which new plants grow. A hard shell or "kernel" holds not only the new plant in embryo, but all the food it needs to nourish it.

- **What is a fruit?**
When scientists talk of fruit they don't just mean apples and pears, but the part of a flower that protects the seed as it ripens and helps spread it. A flower's eggs grow inside its ovaries. Once the eggs are fertilized and turned into seeds, the ovary swells around it into a fruit.

- **Juicy fruit**
Fruit are often juicy and sweet when ripe so that animals are tempted to eat them. The seeds are then spread in the animals' droppings.

The pips inside each grape are seeds from which new grape vines might grow.

Even though they are often very small, such as this bottlebrush of Australia, most trees have flowers.

- **Plums and cherries**
Fruits, such as plums, are called "drupes." They have a fleshy outside and a hard kernel or stone inside protecting the seeds. The stone may be too big for animals to swallow so they eat just the flesh, but the seeds still get spread.

- **False fruit**
Some fruit are called false fruit because they are made from more than just the ovary of the flower. Apples and pears, for example, have the ovary as their core, but their fleshy parts are actually swollen stalk.

- **Legumes**
Peas, beans, and other legumes are soft, dry fruit held in a case called a pod.

▶ Poppies are "annuals" and flower, scatter their seeds, and die in just one year. Buds appear in early summer, then open up as it gets warmer, releasing a flower that is fully grown by midsummer. Once pollinated, their petals wither and fall off, leaving a seed capsule. By fall, the capsule has dried and developed holes, and the ripe seeds can be shaken out by the wind.

1. The fully formed flower is packed inside a bud, enclosed by the green "sepals"

2. Once the weather is warm enough, the bud begins to open

3. The sepals open wider and the petals grow outward and backward

4. The poppy is now fully grown and ready to attract insects. Poppy flowers always have four petals

5. After pollination, the petals fall away, leaving a seed capsule

6. By fall, small holes appear at the top of the dry capsule so seeds can be shaken out

FACTS: About spreading plants

▶ Pollen are the male germ cells that must reach the eggs to fertilize them. They are microscopically small and some are spread by sticking to the legs and bodies of insects drawn to the flower's nectar.

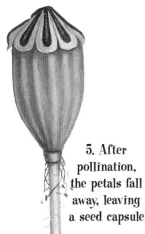

- **Scattered far and wide**
  Plants can't move, but they can spread their pollen and seeds over a wide area. Only a few seeds will grow, so plants usually produce large numbers to ensure their survival.

- **Seed spreading**
  Some seeds are so tiny that they are easily carried by the wind. Others have hooks or hairs on them so that they catch on the fur of passing animals.

Garden & wildflowers

ALL FLOWERS WERE WILD ONCE but through history gardeners have adapted them to the garden by selecting seeds and grafting plants together to bring out particular qualities. Their efforts have created a huge range of beautiful new plants, including roses, carnations, chrysanthemums, tulips, and many more. There are now more than a million kinds of garden flower, although wildflowers are becoming rare as human activity restricts the places where they can grow. Many wildflowers, such as the lady's slipper orchid, are now in danger of becoming extinct.

FACTS: Garden flowers

- **Big and bold**
  On the whole, garden flowers have much bigger flowers in bolder colors than their wild cousins. The wild dog rose has tiny pale pink or white blooms. Garden roses have big blooms in strong colors, from deep red to blue.

- **Cut flowers**
  Once cut flowers could only be bought in the right season. Now they are grown in warm places all year round, such as Colombia, and flown in chilled conditions to bring them fresh to local stores in under two days.

  ▽ *An enormous range of cut flowers can now be brought all year round.*

FACTS: Wild flowers

▶ *The edelweiss survives because it can grow at very high altitude in the Alps, sprouting out from cracks in the rocks. This is because its leaves and blooms are covered in a coat of wooly hairs that protect it from the cold.*

- **Meadows and woodlands**
  Every kind of place has its own kind of wild flower. On heathlands, flowers such as bell-heather, gorse, and scarlet pimpernel grow. In meadows, tiny buttercups, daisies, and clover grow in the grass. In woodlands, flowers such as violets, primroses, and celandines grow. By the sea, sea campion and thrift grow on the rocks, and birdsfoot trefoil on grassy clifftops.

- **Protected flowers**
  Some wildflowers are now so rare that the few survivors must be protected by law. This is true of many orchids.

FACTS: About perennials & biennials

▲ *The giant sunflower is a perennial. It is a native of Peru but is now grown in many places, both for its big yellow flowers and for its seeds, which provide cooking oil.*

- **Annuals**
  Annuals are plants, such as delphiniums, that grow from seeds, flower, disperse their seeds, and die in a single growing season.

- **Biennials**
  Biennials live for two years. In the first, the plant grows leaves on a bulb or taproot, which sustains it with food through the winter. It flowers in the second summer.

- **Perennials**
  Perennials, such as wallflowers and chrysanthemums, live several years, surviving through the winter on underground food stores such as bulbs.

- **Ephemerals**
  Ephemerals, such as groundsel, are short-lived plants that grow from seed, bloom, and die within a few weeks.

▼ *Flowers probably evolved their colorful blooms and beautiful scents to attract the insects they rely on for pollination. But the efforts of gardeners over the centuries have added many new and often spectacular blooms to those created by natural evolution, including roses, tulips, delphiniums, and many more. Many of these new flowers no longer rely on insects for pollination, but are pollinated by humans.*

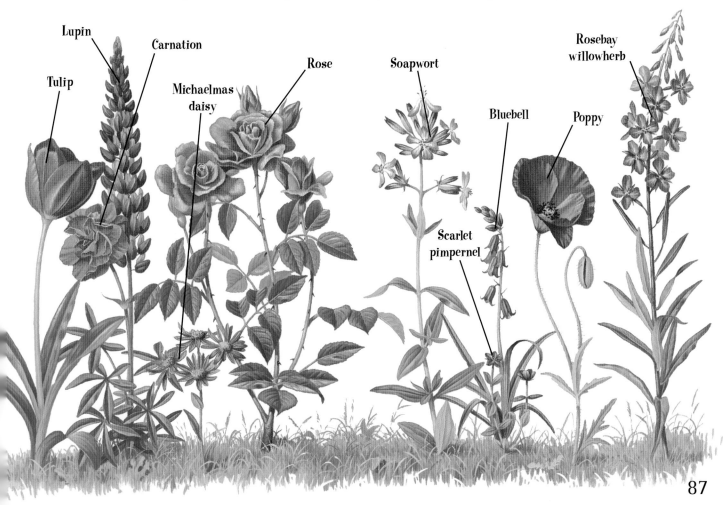

Lupin

Carnation

Tulip

Michaelmas daisy

Rose

Soapwort

Rosebay willowherb

Bluebell

Poppy

Scarlet pimpernel

How trees grow

ALTHOUGH SOME DWARF WILLOWS grow just a few inches high, trees are generally the largest of all plants. Indeed, the giant redwood tree is the biggest of all living things. Trees can grow big because they don't have soft, green "herbaceous" stems like other plants; they have stiff, brown, woody stems, covered in protective bark, that can grow tall and support an enormous weight of leaves. With most trees, there is a single, thick central stem–the trunk–and leaves and side branches only grow some way off the ground–so they are well out of the reach of most browsing animals.

FACTS: About tree trunks

▲ Slicing through a tree's trunk can reveal a lot about its history—its age, the rate at which it has grown, and the conditions it has faced over the years.

- **Inside the trunk**
  The center of a trunk is the dead "heartwood." The living part is the middle—the "sapwood" and the "cambium." Outside is a protective layer of bark.

- **Tree rings**
  Each ring inside the trunk represents a year's growth. Rings close together indicate slow growth; rings far apart indicate rapid growth.

FACTS: About seeds

- **Seed production**
  Because only a small portion of their seeds survive, most trees produce thousands each year.

- **Seed dispersal**
  The seeds of many trees are dispersed by wind, so they are shaped to become airborne easily—maple tree seeds are encased in a pair of flat wings, while willow seeds are shaped like tiny parachutes.

▼ Many trees have seeds that are spread by the wind. The eucalyptus trees of Australia are among the many that have long helicopter-like wings on which they can flutter long distances before they land.

Timber is either hardwood, from broad-leaved trees or softwood, from conifers. Softwood trees are much faster growing (about 33 feet every 30 years) and are grown in huge numbers on plantations in places such as the Rocky Mountains, North America (right). Because they grow faster, these trees provide softer wood. Softwoods are mostly used for making cheap furniture, paper, and for building. Hardwoods are used for more expensive furniture and shipbuilding.

◀ Cedars have smooth, upright cones, which are made up of a lot of closely packed scales, each attached to two seeds. Over a few years these scales gradually break off the cones and fall to the ground, taking their seeds with them.

- **Seed cones**
  The seeds of conifers develop inside hard, protective cones until they are ready.

- **Catkins**
  Oak trees produce male flowers called catkins— long clusters that hang from the branches and release pollen into the air. When the pollen lands on the ovaries of female flowers and fertilizes them, the ovaries develop into acorns.

- **Nuts and berries**
  Some trees have seeds growing inside soft, fleshy fruits, such as berries. Others have them growing inside hard shells, such as acorns and walnuts.

DATA: Trees

- **THE BIGGEST TREE**
  In the world is "General Sherman," a giant sequoia in California–272 feet tall and 82 feet around.

- **THE FASTEST-GROWING TREE**
  The Albizia falcata is a tropical pea tree and can grow 33 feet in 13 months.

- **THE LONGEST LIVING TREE**
  The oldest surviving tree was a bristlecone pine in Nevada, which had lived for 5,100 years.

- **THE LONGEST LIVING SPECIES**
  The oldest surviving species of tree is thought to be the maidenhair tree of China, which first appeared more than 160 million years ago.

Deciduous trees

DECIDUOUS TREES are trees that lose their leaves at some time during the year, usually to cut down their need for water. In cool regions, they lose them in winter because water is hard to come by when groundwater is frozen. In warm regions, they lose them in the summer when the soil dries out quickly. All deciduous trees are flowering plants (see page 84) and have broad, flat leaves, which is why they are also known as broad-leaved trees–although there are also evergreen broad-leaved trees. Broad-leaved trees include deciduous trees, such as ash and chestnut, evergreen trees, such as holly, and palm trees.

FACTS: About palm trees

- **Long leaves**
  Palm trees have thick, tough leaves that help them survive in hot places. There are about 2,800 species, some with leaves as long as 40 feet.

- **No branches**
  Palms have no branches. The leaves grow directly out from the trunk.

▶ *The leaves, stems, and fruit of palm trees provide a lot of useful products, ranging from baskets, furniture, food, and oil. Even soap.*

▼ *In spring, the buds of new leaves shoot on the trees, and slowly open. Flowers appear on the tree, too, and fruit trees blossom. Because plenty of sunlight can still filter down to the ground through the thin canopy of leaves, woodland flowers such as violets bloom beneath the trees.*

▼ *In summer, the leaves on the trees are fully grown, providing a sheltered home for a wide variety of different animals and plants. The dense foliage keeps the woodland beneath at an even temperature—nights are warmer and days are cooler here than out in the open.*

FACTS: About deciduous trees

• **Tree life**
Oaks and other trees can live up to 500 years. Some elms that reproduce from suckers never really die at all because the trees are constantly renewing themselves, creating a whole grove of their offshoots.

• **Fallen trees**
Every now and then, trees die and fall over. As they crash to the floor, they open up the woodland floor to the sky, creating a glade where new trees and other plants thrive.

△ *Deciduous forests once covered the whole of Europe, but now only fragments of these great forests remain.*

• **Oak trees**
There are 450 species of oak tree, some deciduous, some evergreen. But all grow from acorns.

• **Dutch elm disease**
Elm trees were once common in northern Europe, but many have been killed by Dutch elm disease—a fungus whose spores are spread by beetles that live in the bark.

• **Coppicing**
Many European woodlands have long been managed by foresters. Trees, such as willows, are cut off at the trunk, or "coppiced." The new straight shoots that grow from the top make "withies," which are good for basketmaking.

▽ *By fall, the days are getting colder and there is less water available. To survive, the trees must prepare to lose their leaves. The chlorophyll that makes the leaves green starts to break down and sugars in the leaves gradually turn them brown, red, or orange.*

▽ *As winter approaches, the trees get ready to close down altogether. The leaves that changed color in the fall start to drop off, leaving the trees bare and dormant. During this time, winter buds develop, containing new leaves, which will burst open the following spring.*

Conifers and cycads

CONIFERS, AND THEIR TROPICAL RELATIVES cycads and gingkos, are among the oldest of all kinds of plants. They first appeared more than 300 million years ago, long before the age of dinosaurs. Conifers, cycads, and gingkos are all called gymnosperms, and make their seeds in cones. Conifers are tall, mostly evergreen trees that generally grow in cool and mountainous regions. A few cypresses are the only tropical conifers. Cycads, however, are tropical trees that look like stubby palm trees. Gingkos or maidenhair trees are tall trees with fan-shaped leaves that grow only in eastern China.

FACTS: About coniferous forests

Like all conifers, pine trees have long needles and cones. They also grow tall and fast and are fully grown in under 20 years, which is why they provide three quarters of the world's lumber.

• **Cold resistance**
Conifers are able to survive in cold areas with little water because instead of leaves they have thin waxy needles that shed snow easily and lose very little water. (Water cannot be used by trees when it is frozen). Their tall, narrow shape helps shed snow, too.

• **Evergreen**
Nearly all conifers are evergreen, which means that their leaves stay on all year round. Larches are an exception—their needles fall off in fall.

• **Plantations**
In various cold regions of the world conifers are grown in narrowly planted rows on massive plantations to provide lumber. They are fast-growing and can also survive on soil that is too poor for other crops.

• **Life in a coniferous forest**
Coniferous forests are usually quite dense and dark, and so there is much less other plant life beneath the trees than there is in a deciduous forest (see page 90)—usually just fungi, ferns, and lichen.

• **Boreal forest**
The most extensive coniferous forests are found in the colder, northern parts of the world—mostly North America, Scandinavia, and Siberia.

• **Tree mix**
Most coniferous forests are made up of conifers, such as pines, spruces, and firs.

• **Pine family**
Pines make up the largest family of conifers. This includes almost 100 different species, such as the Scots pine, Corsican pine, and the white pine.

FACTS: Seeds and cones

- **Cone bearers**
  Instead of flowers, conifers and cycads have male and female cones that produce and carry seeds.

- **Male cones**
  The smaller male cones grow in clusters and produce pollen grains which travel on the wind to fertilize the female cones.

- **Female cones**
  Once fertilized, female cones may take as long as three years to develop their seeds.

- **Female scales**
  Each scale of the female cone has one or more seeds attached to it. As they develop they are protected within the hard cone. When they are ready, the scales open up and either release the seeds or fall away from the cone, taking the seeds with them.

▲ *Cones are very sensitive to changes in the dampness of the air. In dry weather, the scales shrivel and stand out stiffly. When it is damper, they absorb the moisture and close up neatly again.*

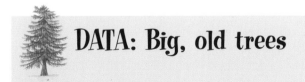

▲ *The giant redwood, or sequoia, trees of Sierra Nevada in California are the world's largest living things, growing 300 feet or more tall. Some are among the oldest, too. Some redwoods date back to before the days of the Ancient Egyptians, 4,000 years ago.*

DATA: Big, old trees

- **THE TALLEST LIVING TREE**
  The tallest tree in the world is a coast redwood in Humboldt Redwoods State Park, California—370 feet.

- **THE OLDEST LIVING TREE**
  Is a 5,100-year-old bristlecone pine in California's White Mt.

- **THE BIGGEST FOREST**
  Is in Siberia—6.5 million square miles (17 million sq km).

Mosses and ferns

NOT ALL PLANTS GROW FROM SEEDS. The very first plants to grow on land some 400 million years ago grew from tiny, dustlike cells called spores. These ancient plants, including mosses, liverworts, club mosses, horsetails, and ferns, still survive today, although none of them ever grow as big as they did in the time before seed-bearing plants appeared some 200 million years ago. They love damp, shady places, and they are often seen carpeting rocks along streams and growing all over trees in moist woodlands and steamy tropical rain forests—sometimes far above the ground.

FACTS: About ferns

- **Roots, leaves, and stems**
  Unlike mosses, ferns are "pteridophytes," or featherplants, and have roots and leaves, and veins to take food and water up and down inside the stem. Fern leaves are called fronds.

- **Tree ferns**
  Tree ferns can grow up to 80 feet tall, and they are abundant in moist tropical rain forests. They have no branches, and the fronds grow in a crown from the top of the trunk.

- **Passenger plants**
  Some ferns, such as bird's-nest fern and stag's horn fern, grow on other plants without harming them. They get their moisture by collecting dripping rainwater.

- **Horsetails**
  Horsetails are similar to ferns, but they belong to a group called sphenophytes. Although nowadays most are small, these plants grew more than 100 feet tall in the Carboniferous Period 300-355 million years ago.

▶ *Ferns grow from spores made on the underside of their leaves. The spores form a prothallus, which creates the embryo for a new fern to grow from.*

Sporangia are where the fern makes spores

In each sori, there are sacs called sporangia

On the underside of leaves are balls called sori

The root and stem grow to form a new fern frond

A new root and stem grow and the prothallus dies away

FACTS: About moss

- **Moss**
  Mosses and liverworts make up a group of their own called bryophytes. They form in thin cushions on walls, rocks, and old logs and have no true roots, so they have to draw their moisture from the air through their stems and tiny threads called rhizoids. This is why they like damp places, such as riverbanks.

- **Sponges**
  Sphagnum moss lives in bogs and can soak up to 25 times its own weight in water. It is the main constituent in peat bogs in Ireland and Scotland.

- **New moss**
  Moss spores make male and female cells, which swim together to create the embryo for a new moss.

Spores burst from the sporangia and spread on the wind

Settling in a suitable place, the spore puts out shoots

The shoots form a heart-shaped plant or prothallus, which makes male and female cells

The male cells fertilize the female

When it rains, male cells swim to the female cells

The embryo of a new plant grows in the prothallus.

▲ *Ferns are by far the biggest group of spore-bearing plants and there are about 12,000 different kinds. Unlike all the other spore-bearing plants, they have big leaves called fronds. Fronds can grow to an enormous size. The fronds of the Marattia can grow more than 23 feet long. Technically, fronds are called megaphyllous leaves, which just means big spore bearers.*

Fungi and mushrooms

FUNGI AND MUSHROOMS grow in the ground like plants, but they are not plants at all. Fungi and mushrooms, along with toadstools, yeast, mildew, and mold (like the mold on bread), all belong to a special group of organisms called Myceteae. Unlike plants, fungi have no green chlorophyll, so they cannot make their own food. So they have to get their food in other ways. Many fungi are parasites, which means they feed off living animals, plants, and other organisms. Others are "saprophytes," which means they live off the remains of dead plants and animals.

▶ *Fungi are both good and bad for us. Some kinds of fungi, such as mushrooms and cheese mold, are good to eat, but others are deadly poisonous. Some grow on plants and animals and make them ill, such as the aspergillus mold. Others provide antibiotic drugs. Yeast helps bread rise and beer ferment.*

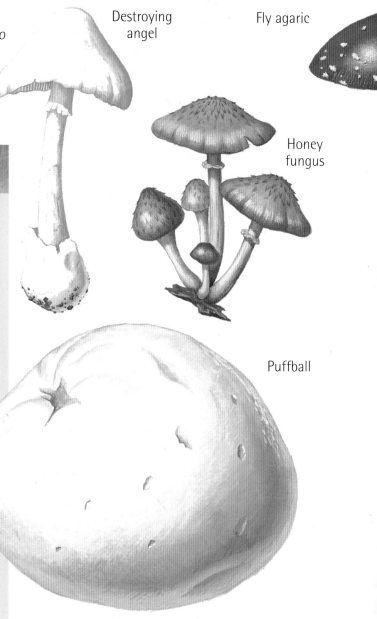

Destroying angel

Fly agaric

Honey fungus

Puffball

FACTS: About parasites

▲ *Fungi live off other organisms. These fungi are growing on a tree, clinging on with hundreds of cottonlike threads, called hyphae, which digest and absorb materials from the tree.*

• **Chemical rotters**
Fungi rot the organism they are feeding on by sending out special chemicals, called enzymes, which break down plant and animal cells.

• **Food source**
Fungi absorb food from the rotting organism.

• **Blue cheese**
The enzymes released by mold are what give blue cheese its flavor—and make bread mold toxic.

FACTS: What fungi are made of

- **Spreading threads**
Fungi are made of cottonlike threads, called hyphae, which spread out in a tangled mass through the soil—or into the tissues of the plant or animal the fungi are living on.

◄ *Sometimes, hyphae (pronounced hi-fi) bundle together to form what are called fruiting bodies—such as mushrooms and toadstools. But they can also make tiny pinheads, such as the mold on rotting fruit.*

Shaggy ink cap

Field mushroom

Oyster mushroom

Death cap

FACTS: Poisonous fungi

- **Fly agaric**
Fly agaric makes the poison muscarine, which causes stomach pains and convulsions, and can occasionally kill. Fly agaric was once taken in small doses for its hallucinatory effect.

- **Death cap**
The death cap and destroying angel toadstools look quite like harmless mushrooms—but they are deadly. Death cap contains the poisons amanitine and phalloidine, which can kill a human within six hours of eating it, due to kidney and liver failure.

- **False morel**
False morel makes the poison gyromitrin which can create terrible stomach pains.

▶ *Fly agaric announces its deadly poison with its bright color. Eating even small amounts can completely knock you out.*

97

Algae

A KIND OF ALGAE was among the first living things to appear on Earth some three billion years ago. There are now many different kinds of algae, and although some are tiny, they are very important. They grow almost everywhere there is water, from the oceans to damp walls. Algae in the oceans not only provide food for creatures, such as whales, but maintain the levels of oxygen in the air–and without this we could not breathe. Algae can draw energy from sunlight like most plants, but they have no leaves, stems, roots, or flowers. Indeed, many scientists don't put algae in the plant kingdom at all but in their own kingdom called *Protoctista*.

FACTS: About lichens

◀ Lichens grow on bare rock, and can often be seen on stone walls and old stone buildings. But they are very sensitive to any pollution in the air—especially sulfur dioxide from coal-fired power stations—and will not grow where the air is dirty.

▼ Lichens grow in three kinds of shapes. Crusty or "crustose" lichens grow in disks on stones and walls. Leafy or "foliose" lichens grow on the ground or on trees, and their edges curl up like leaves. Shrubby or "fruticose" lichens look like tiny bushes.

Crustose lichen

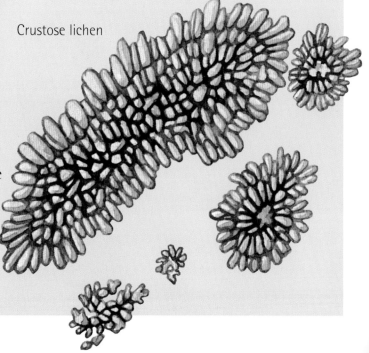

- **Algae and fungi**
  Lichens look like plants. But they are actually a remarkable partnership between algae and fungi. The algae are tiny green balls, and use sunlight to make food for the fungi. The fungi create a protective blanket above and below and act as a water store.

- **Reindeer food**
  The algae-fungi partnership enables lichens to live on bare rock faces and very harsh places, such as the Antarctic and on mountaintops. If things get too dry or cold, they simply go into suspended animation, ready for the good times to begin again. Some lichens provide the only food for reindeer in the Arctic.

FACTS: About seaweed

- **Large algae**
  Seaweeds are very large algae that grow on seashores, or get washed up on beaches. They are usually brown, red, or green in color. They tend to grow in the shallows because they need sunlight.

- **Brown and red**
  Brown algae such as kelp grow 50-65 feet down. Red algae grow 100-200 feet down.

- **Holding on**
  Seaweeds have a "holdfast," which looks like a mass of roots, but is just the seaweed's suckers for holding onto rocks despite crashing waves. They actually rely on the water to support them.

- **Natural floats**
  Some seaweeds have air-filled bladders to help them float near the surface.

- **Useful weeds**
  In many places, seaweed is gathered from the seashore to put on the land as fertilizer. It is also a valuable source of iodine and some antibiotics. "Alginates" from seaweeds help set ice cream.

Seaweed helps oxygenate the water and provides grazing for many sea creatures

- **Sea food**
  Seaweed may not look appetizing, but it is popular in Chinese and Japanese cooking. The red seaweed Porphyra is used in Wales to make a kind of dessert called "laver-bread."

FACTS: About algae

- **Plankton**
  In the oceans, the most important plants are "phytoplankton"—tiny organisms that float in in the surface waters of the oceans and grow in huge numbers. These are food for a wide range of sea creatures.

- **Algal bloom**
  Sometimes algae grow in such huge numbers that they choke other life. These "algal blooms" can sometimes be caused in rivers by fertilizer pollution from farms.

▶ *Most seaweeds stay submerged all the time, but many have to cope with the tides—and long periods when they are left high and dry out of water. Some can survive almost a day in baking sunshine, drying up, then returning to life when the tide comes in and refreshes them again. In fact, seaweeds are banded in the tide zone according to how long they can live out of water.*

Plants for food

PLANTS PROVIDE the "staple" (basic or essential) food for most people around the world, and an area one and a half times the size of the United States is used for growing crops. More than 12,000 species of plant have been used for food at one time or other, but only about 150 or so are regularly grown as crops, including cereals, such as wheat, rice, and corn; fruit, such as oranges and bananas; root vegetables, such as potatoes and yams; green vegetables, such as cabbage and kale; and legumes such as soybeans and lentils. Some of these were first cultivated more than 10,000 years ago.

FACTS: Fruit and vegetables

- **Citrus fruit**
  Oranges, lemons, grapefruits, tangerines, and limes are citrus fruit and are grown in huge quantities in places with Mediterranean climates. The fruit are picked in winter and often made into juice.

- **Fruit farms**
  Apples are grown in orchards, oranges are grown in groves, and bananas on plantations.

- **Potato blight**
  Potatoes come originally from South America, but they became the staple for poor Irish farmers in the 19th century. When the potato crop was ruined by a disease called "blight" in the 1840s, millions of Irish people starved.

▶ Bananas are the major export of many countries in Central America, such as El Salvador and Honduras. They are picked while still green and semi-frozen for export by sea.

Millet is grown in dry places, such as Africa, and is ground to make flour

Sunflower seeds are crushed to produce oil

▶ These are just some of the plants grown for food. Many, including sunflowers, corn, and olives are made into oil. The cereals can be ground to make flour, but rice is usually cooked as whole grains, while corn, millet, and sorghum (as well as oats) are typically made into a kind of porridge. Corn comes in two kinds. One gives the large head with a lot of grains, known as sweetcorn or corn on the cob. Corn with a smaller head and smaller grains is used for corn oil or corn starch.

Olives grow on trees in Mediterranean areas. They are eaten whole or pressed to make oil

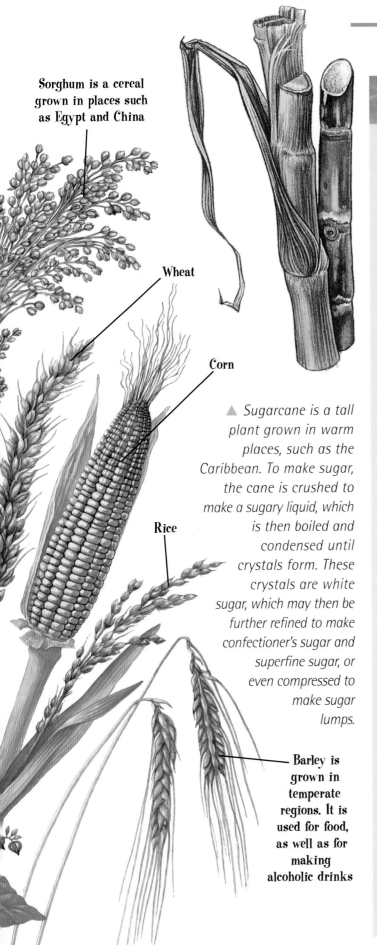

Sorghum is a cereal grown in places such as Egypt and China

Wheat

Corn

Rice

▲ Sugarcane is a tall plant grown in warm places, such as the Caribbean. To make sugar, the cane is crushed to make a sugary liquid, which is then boiled and condensed until crystals form. These crystals are white sugar, which may then be further refined to make confectioner's sugar and superfine sugar, or even compressed to make sugar lumps.

Barley is grown in temperate regions. It is used for food, as well as for making alcoholic drinks

FACTS: About cereals

- **What are cereals?**
  Cereals are crops, such as wheat, corn, rice, oats, rye, and barley. They are all grasses and we eat the seeds or grain, leaving the stalks and leaves to rot into animal food called silage.

- **Wheat**
  Wheat provides the basic food for over one in three people in the world. Wheat grain is ground to make flour, which is then used to make things, such as bread and pasta.

- **Rice**
  Widely grown in southern Asia, rice is the staple food for half the world's population. In China alone, 200 million tons are grown every year. There are more than 14,000 types, including many long-grain rices, such as Basmati rice used with Indian curries, medium-grain rices used for Italian risotto, and short-grain rice used for desserts. Brown rice is white rice with the husk on.

- **Paddy fields**
  Rice is the only cereal crop grown in water—in flooded fields called "paddies." Most of the work in producing it is done by hand. There are typically three crops a year.

▶ Before processing, rice grains are enclosed in tough husks. Removing this outer layer makes brown rice; refining the grains even further makes white rice.

Herbs and spices

 HERBS AND SPICES HAVE BEEN used to flavor food and to make medicines since prehistoric times. Herbs are small flowering plants, and there are hundreds of different kinds, each with its own special properties. Usually it is the leaves that are valued, but it can be the flowers or the stem. Some, such as basil and oregano, are edible and used in small quantities to flavor food. Others, like feverfew, are valued more for their medicinal qualities. Spices are strongly flavored seeds, roots, and bark that are usually ground into powder to add to food as it is cooked.

FACTS: About tea and coffee

- **Tea**
Tea is the dried leaves of a small camellia bush that grows on hillsides in subtropical areas, especially in India and Sri Lanka, Japan, and China. The best tea grows slowly at high altitudes (up to 6,600 feet in places).

- **Black tea and green tea**
There are two main kinds of tea: green tea and black tea. Green tea is picked and dried quickly, providing a mild flavor. Green tea is popular in China. Black tea is only partly dried before it is crushed in rolling machines, providing a much stronger flavor. Black tea is preferred in Europe.

- **Coffee**
Coffee is made from the ground and roasted beans of the coffee bush. The beans are collected and soaked, then the husks are removed and the beans are dried, sorted, and roasted. The longer the roast, the stronger and darker the coffee.

- **Instant coffee**
Coffee can be made into instant coffee powder by boiling coffee dry, or into instant coffee granules by plunging ground beans into liquid gas to freeze-dry them.

◄ *For tea, tea pickers—mainly women—neatly pluck the young tips of the leaves by hand and put them in baskets slung over their shoulders.*

◄ *Coffee grows in the tropics in places, such as Brazil. The best is grown on slopes 2,000-6,000 feet up. Coffee beans are not actually beans at all, but a kind of berry, and are bright red when on the bush.*

FACTS: About herbs

• **Herbal drugs**
Many of today's medicines came originally from plants, including aspirin (from willow trees), morphine (from the seeds of the opium poppy), and quinine (from the bark of the cinchona tree of South America). An extract of the rosy periwinkle, called vincristine, is one of the drugs used against leukemia, a childhood cancer.

• **Herb facts**
Egyptian pyramid builders ate garlic because they thought it would give them strength...rosemary gets its name from the Latin *ros marinus* which means "sea dew"...bay leaves were used to crown poets and heroes in Ancient Rome...the Ancient Greeks called basil "King of Herbs"...the Latin name for sage is *Salvia*, which means healthy, and sage is thought to have healing qualities...mint and the spice cinnamon keep moths away from clothes...oregano is used as a dye, as well as a food flavor.

Opium poppy flower

Opium poppy seed head

Foxglove

White willow

Periwinkle

FACTS: About spices

• **Spice facts**
It takes 182,000 hand-picked crocus flower heads to make one pound of saffron...ginger is the root of a tall grasslike plant that is harvested after flowering...chili can actually cool you down because it makes you sweat...cinnamon comes from the bark of a tree...nutmeg is the seed of a tree...star anise takes 15 years to grow.

• **Spice islands**
Many spices come from the Moluccas in Indonesia, which were once known as the Spice Islands.

◀ *This shows just a few of the many herbs and flowers valued for medicinal purposes. Foxglove in large doses is poisonous, but it yields the drug digitalis, used in small doses to treat heart problems. Feverfew was once thought an effective treatment for fever.*

Feverfew

103

Tropical plants

The tropics are warm nearly all the time, and in the rain forests there is abundant moisture. The combination creates almost ideal conditions for plant growth, and tropical forests are not only lush but contain an astonishing variety of plants–including some of the world's most spectacular and strange. The rain forests are the world's richest plant habitats, containing more than 40 percent of the world's plant species. No one knows exactly how many different plants there are. But botanists counted more than 180 species of tree alone in one hectare of the Malaysian forest.

FACTS: Coping with drought

- **Deep roots**
  When there is no water on the surface, plants can often find moisture deep underground by growing long roots. Mesquite roots often grow as deep as 33 feet, and may be as long as 165 feet.

- **Tough leaves**
  In moist places, plants lose water by evaporation from their leaves. So desert plants usually have tough, waxy leaves that cut moisture loss to a minimum—and have as few leaves as possible.

The baobab of Africa and Australia survives in dry places by retaining moisture in its barrel-shaped trunk, which can be up to 30 feet thick.

- **Cacti**
  Cacti live in American deserts. They have no leaves and a thick skin, so water loss is cut to a minimum. Their fat stems can hold huge amounts of water, which is why they are called succulents.

- **Prickly plants**
  Lush vegetation is so rare in deserts that animals eat anything. So cacti, prickly pears, and thorn bushes grow prickles to protect themselves.

Cacti have to pollinate, just like every other flowering plant, and so every few years they produce big colorful blooms in order to attract insects quickly.

FACTS: About tropical water plants

• **Amazon lily**
The world's biggest water plant is the Amazon water lily. Its massive floating leaves grow up to 6 feet across, and can sometimes support the weight of a child.

• **Water hyacinth**
The water hyacinth is the world's fastest growing water plant—so fast growing that it is thought of as a pest, especially because it chokes waterways and encourages mosquitoes.

Rafflesia has no stem—just a huge flower that sits on the ground

◄ *The Rafflesia of Southeast Asia is the world's biggest flower. A single bloom can be up to 3 feet across. It smells like rotting meat—perhaps to attract the flies it needs to help it pollinate.*

Key facts: Plants

Parts of a flower

There are two kinds of flowering plants: Monocotyledons and Dicotyledons. Monocotyledons have one leaf sprout, e.g. grasses, cereals, tulips, and daffodils. Dicotyledons have two leaf sprouts, e.g. most deciduous trees, vegetables, and fruit. Pollen is made in the "anthers" on top of the stamens, the male parts of the flower. The female part, or pistil, is topped by a sticky "stigma," which traps the pollen. A long tube or "style" takes it down to the ovary, where it meets the eggs to create the seeds.

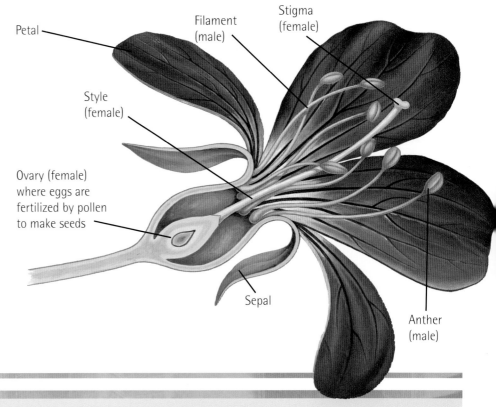

Petal

Filament (male)

Stigma (female)

Style (female)

Ovary (female) where eggs are fertilized by pollen to make seeds

Sepal

Anther (male)

Plant

- Fossils show that the first plants appeared on Earth more than 1 billion years ago. They lived in the ocean and probably looked like small lumps of green slime.
- Gradually, these earliest plants developed into larger algae, or seaweeds.
- About 400 million years ago, small mosslike plants spread slowly on to the rocky, empty land.
- By 300 million years ago, ferns grew as big as trees, forming steamy, swampy prehistoric forests.
- Some 200 million years ago, forests of conifer trees spread across the land, as the first dinosaurs roamed among them.
- Flowering plants appeared about 130 million years ago, bringing bright colors to the landscape.

The Plant Kingdom

Scientific group name	Ordinary name	Approx. number of different species
Algae	Seaweeds	6,000
Bryophytes	Mosses	10,000
	Liverworts	14,000
Pteridophytes	Ferns	12,000
	Horsetails	30
	Clubmosses	400
Gymnosperms	Conifers	600
Angiosperms	Flowering plants	250,000 +

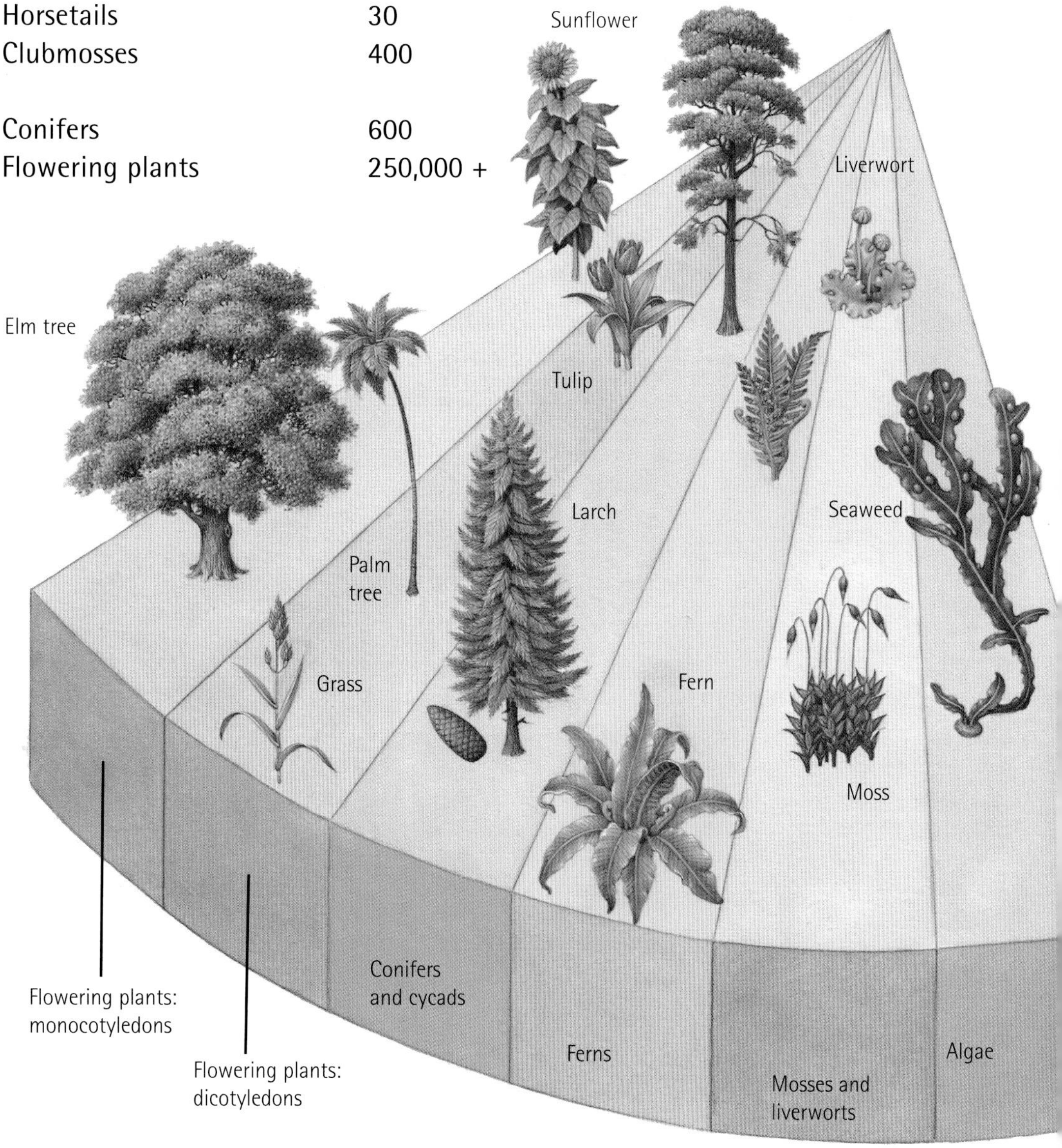

Fungi

1. Rusts and mildews
2. Molds
3. Sac fungi
4. Club fungi
5. Imperfect fungi
6. Slime molds

Sunflower

Liverwort

Elm tree

Tulip

Seaweed

Larch

Palm tree

Fern

Grass

Moss

Flowering plants: monocotyledons

Flowering plants: dicotyledons

Conifers and cycads

Ferns

Algae

Mosses and liverworts

Key facts: Plants

Plant records

- **The smallest plant**
  The smallest plant is the duckweed Wolffia arrhiza, which has fronds less than $^{1}/_{25}$ inch across.

- **The biggest plant**
  The biggest plant is the Giant Sequioa tree called General Sherman in California, which is 272 feet tall.

- **The oldest living thing**
  The oldest living thing is a lichen in Antarctica thought to be over 10,000 years old.

- **Tallest tree ever measured**
  A eucalyptus in Victoria, Australia, was 470 feet tall.

- **The biggest flower**
  The biggest flower is the Rafflesia of Indonesia, which has blooms more than 3 feet across.

- **The biggest water plant**
  The biggest water plant is the Amazon water lily, which has leaves more than 6 feet across.

- **The biggest leaves**
  The biggest leaves belong to the raffia palm; they can grow up to 60 feet long.

- **The deepest roots**
  The deepest roots belong to a fig tree growing in South Africa, which has roots down more than 394 feet.

- **The biggest seed**
  The biggest seed is the coco de mer coconut, which weighs up to 40 pounds.

- **The fastest growing plant**
  The fastest growing plant is the bamboo, which can grow up to 35 inches in a single day.

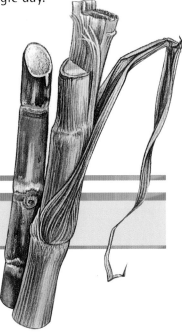

Some major food crops

CEREALS	SUGAR	VEGETABLES	NONFOOD PLANTS
Wheat	Sugarcane	Tomatoes	Trees for
Rice	Beet	Squash	timber and
Corn			paper
Barley	**FRUITS AND**	**LEAVES**	Cotton
Oats	**NUTS**	Lettuce	Tobacco
Rye	Apples	Cabbage	Rubber
	Oranges		Jute
ROOT CROPS	Bananas	**HERBS AND**	Coir
Potatoes	Grapes	**SPICES**	Flax
Yams	Mangoes	Parsley	Sisal
Cassava	Melons	Basil	Kapok
Manioc	Blueberries	Chili	Hops
	Hazelnuts	Chocolate	
	Peanuts		

Plants also provide 80% of all our fuels. The main fossil fuels are coal, oil, and natural gas.

Plant environments

Temperate woodlands
Deciduous
- trees, such as beeches, birches, hickories, maples, oaks, poplars, and walnuts
- shrubs, such as brambles, hawthorn, and honeysuckle
- woodland flowers, such as violets, primroses, foxgloves, willowherbs, and anenomes

Coniferous
- trees, such as redwoods, giant sequoias, Douglas firs, cedars, and pines
- small trees, such as rowan and hazel
- ferns
- bilberries

Grasslands
- grasses, such as tussock, marram, meadow, and rye
- trees and shrubs, such as acacia, thorn, baobab, and rokerboom

- flowers, such as vetches, trefoils, orchids, blazing star, worts, and coneflowers

Tropical forests
- trees, such as mahoganies, teaks, banyans, and palms
- lichens
- vines and lianas
- epiphytes, such as orchids, ferns, tree ferns, and bromeliads
- carnivorous plants, such as Venus fly traps and pitcher plants

Lakes and rivers
- reeds, rushes, and papyrus
- sedges
- worts, such as bladderwort and fanwort
- water crowfoot
- waterlilies and irises
- water hyacinths

Deserts
- cacti
- creosote bushes, thorn trees, quiver trees, Joshua trees, sagebrush, yuccas, and prickly pear
- window plants and pebble plants
- palm trees
- evening primrose

High mountains
- rowan and dwarf willow, crowberries, and bilberries
- wild flowers, such as alpine bluebells, mountain avens, gentian, edelweiss, snowbells, saxifrage, and saussurea
- grasses and mosses

Quiz: Plants

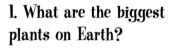

1. What are the biggest plants on Earth?

2. Irises grow from thick stems that grow sideways underground: true or false?

3. What kind of plant is an angiosperm?

4. Why are fruit often juicy and sweet?

5. Seaweeds are a kind of algae: true or false?

6. Which part of a plant draws up water from the ground?

7. Some plants take their food from other plants, rather than from the earth: true or false?

8. Some ferns can grow up to 80 feet tall: true or false?

9. Plants need to absorb something through their leaves in order to turn carbon dioxide from the air and hydrogen from water into food. What do they need to absorb?

10. The giant sequoia tree in California is the world's biggest living thing. It is 505 feet tall: true or false?

11. What is the seed of the oak tree called?

12. The tubes that carry water up a plant's stem are called xylophones: true or false?

13. The oldest surviving species of tree comes from China and first appeared more than 160 million years ago. What is the tree called?

14. Potatoes originally came from Ireland: true or false?

15. What part of the sunflower plant is sunflower oil made from?

16. It takes 182,000 crocus flower heads to make one pound of saffron (a spice used to flavor rice in cooking): true or false?

17. What important food crop is grown in water-filled fields in southern Asia?

18. Lichen growing in Antarctica may be the world's oldest living thing. It is thought to be more than 10,000 years old: true or false?

19. The leaves of the Amazon water lily are more than 6 feet across: true or false?

20. Do pine trees lose their leaves in winter?

Answers:

1. Trees
2. True
3. A flowering plant
4. So that animals are tempted to eat them and spread the seeds in their droppings
5. True
6. The roots
7. True
8. True
9. Sunlight
10. False—it is 272 feet tall
11. Acorn
12. False—they are called xylem
13. The maidenhair tree
14. False—they came from South America
15. The seeds of the sunflower
16. True
17. Rice
18. True
19. True
20. No

THE UNIVERSE

Planet Earth

THIRD PLANET OUT FROM THE SUN, our Earth looks from a distance like a great round blue jewel hanging in the darkness of space. It is blue because three-quarters of its rocky surface is drowned under blue ocean waters, which shimmer in the light of the Sun. No other planet has this much water on its surface. Here and there, its rocky surface pokes up above the water to form half a dozen large continents and thousands of smaller islands. The very ends of the world are glistening white–the polar ice caps.

FACTS: Earth measurements

- **The size of the Earth**
  The distance around the Earth is 24,815 miles at the equator. It's diameter at the equator is 7,910 miles—larger than its diameter pole to pole, by 27 miles.

- **The weight of the Earth**
  The Earth weighs 6,000 trillion trillion tons.

- **The angle of the Earth**
  The Earth tilts over at an angle of 23.45°.

▼ *Satellites have allowed the Earth to be measured more accurately then ever before. Satellites can detect movements of the continents of just a fingernail's width or small variations in the height of the sea's surface.*

▲ *The Earth looks round, but it is not a perfect sphere. Because it spins faster at the equator than the poles, it is actually shaped more like a tangerine, bulging slightly at the equator and flattened at the poles. So scientists used to describe its shape as an oblate spheroid (flattened ball). Now satellite measurements have detected other slight irregularities, so they call it a geoid, which simply means Earth-shaped.*

FACTS: Inside the Earth

- **Probing the Earth**
  Scientists have worked out what the Earth's interior is like from vibrations from earthquakes and underground explosions.

- **Crust**
  The Earth has a thin shell of solid rock called the crust, which varies from 3–7 miles under the oceans to 18–42 miles under the continents.

- **Mantle**
  Beneath the crust is a layer almost 2,000 miles deep, called the mantle. It is so hot here that the rock flows very, very slowly.

- **Core**
  Below the mantle is a core of metal, mostly iron and nickel.

- **Outer core**
  The outer portion of the core is so ferociously hot that the metal is always molten.

- **Inner core**
  The Earth's inner core is even hotter—up to 12,600°F—but the metal here is solid because pressures here are so great that metal simply cannot melt.

Inner core   Outer core   Mantle   Crust

▲ *Earth has several different layers because the materials it is made of have separated out over billions of years. Dense metals, such as iron, sank to the center to form the core, while lighter rock-forming materials floated to the top to form the crust.*

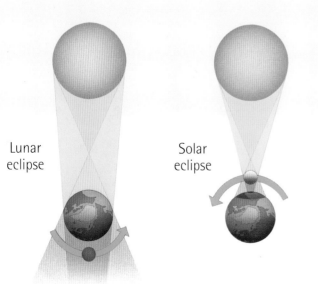

Lunar eclipse

Solar eclipse

◀ *Every now and then, the Earth and Moon get in between each other and the Sun. This is called an eclipse because the planet in between "eclipses," or blocks out, the Sun. A lunar eclipse is when the Moon goes behind the Earth into its shadow. A solar eclipse is when the Moon comes in between the Sun and the Earth, casting a shadow a few miles wide on the Earth.*

The Moon

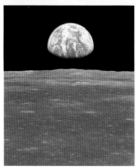

Earthrise on the Moon

THE MOON IS THE BIGGEST, BRIGHTEST object in the night sky. It seems to shine almost like a pale sun. But it does not give out any light itself. It is just a big, cold ball of rock and shines only because it reflects sunlight. The Moon is the Earth's companion in space, and circles round it continuously, just as the Earth circles the Sun. The Moon is about one-quarter of the Earth's size and was probably formed shortly after the Earth, perhaps from hot splashes flung out as a small planet collided with the Earth.

FACTS: About the Moon

- **Pitted surface**
  The Moon's surface is pitted with craters—dents created by the impact of huge rocks early in its history.

- **Seas on the Moon**
  All over the Moon's surface are dark patches that people once believed were seas. In fact, they are not seas at all, but vast plains formed by lava flowing from volcanoes that erupted early in the Moon's history.

- **"Moonths"**
  The word month comes from the Moon, and the time it takes to go once around the Earth. It takes the Moon 27.3 days to circle the Earth, but it actually takes 29.53 days from one full moon to the next, because the Earth moves as well, and the Moon falls a little behind. This 29.53 days cycle is called a lunar month. However, the length of our calendar months was decided a few centuries ago by the Pope.

- **Watery Moon**
  In 1998, X-ray cameras on a NASA space probe revealed that there are huge quantities of water on the Moon, in the form of ice under the Moon's surface.

The moon's rocky mantle is cool and solid, unlike the Earth's mantle

The Moon's outer core is probably solid metal

The Moon has a small inner core of molten metal

▲ *The Moon's surface is very dead compared with the Earth. It has no atmosphere. The surface is just fine white dust, pitted with craters. Also, its rocky interior is cool, not hot like the Earth's, and the volcanic activity that constantly changes the Earth's surface has long since died out on the Moon.*

▲ *The Moon is the only world beyond ours that people have visited. When Neil Armstrong set foot on it on July 21, 1969, he said famously, "That's one small step for man, one giant leap for mankind."*

FACTS: On the Moon

- **Men on the Moon**
  The first men to land on the Moon were Neil Armstrong and Buzz Aldrin—in July 1969. The most recent was Eugene Cernan in 1972.

- **High jumping**
  The Moon's gravity is only a sixth of the Earth's, so everything is very light. Moon astronauts can jump easily—even in heavy space suits.

- **Footprints forever**
  Because there is no air, the sky on the Moon is inky black even in daytime, and there is no wind to ruffle the dust. So the footprints left by the first men on the Moon will be there forever.

- **Day and night**
  Each day on the Moon lasts 360 hours, and the temperature reaches 260°F—but the night is just as long and temperatures plunge to -260°F.

The phases of the Moon

Only the part of the Moon lit by the Sun is bright enough for us to see. But as it circles the Earth, the Sun shines on the Moon from changing angles, and we see more or less of the moon at different times—and so the Moon appears to change shape over the course of a month as it circles the Earth. These changes are called phases.

▼ *During the first half of the month, the Moon grows from a crescent shaped new Moon, to a half-circle shaped half Moon, to a full Moon. This is called waxing. In the second half, it gets smaller or "wanes" through a half Moon back to a crescent-shaped old Moon— curving the opposite way from the new Moon.*

The Sun

THE SUN IS OUR LOCAL STAR, a vast fiery spinning ball of hot gases—three quarters hydrogen and one-quarter helium. It is well over a million times as big as the Earth. The gigantic mass of the Sun creates immense pressures in its core. Such huge pressures fuse hydrogen atoms together in a continual nuclear reaction that boosts temperatures to 27 billion°F (15 billion°C). This heat turns the outer surface of the Sun into a raging inferno that burns so brightly that it completely floodlights the Earth, more than 900,000 miles (1.5 million km) away.

FACTS: Inside the sun

- **A bomb in the heart**
  Pressures in the Sun's core are two trillion times the pressure of the Earth's atmosphere. These fuse so many hydrogen atoms together that it is as if 100 billion nuclear bombs were going off each second.

- **All down to Einstein**
  We owe our understanding of how the Sun produces heat and light to the famous scientist Albert Einstein (1897-1955), who showed how mass can be changed into energy.

- **Surface layers**
  The visible surface layer of the Sun is the photosphere. Above this lies the chromosphere and the corona.

- **Hot surface**
  Temperatures at the surface of the Sun are a phenomenal 10,800°F (6,000°C), enough to melt almost anything. This unimaginable heat accounts for the Sun's brightness.

- **The Sun's age**
  The Sun probably formed about 5 billion years ago, just a little before the Earth, which formed from the debris left over. It will burn out in about 5 billion years' time.

- **The Solar wind**
  Streaming out from the Sun every second are a million tons of electrically charged particles. Earth is protected from this lethal stream, called the solar wind, by its magnetic field.

- **SOHO**
  The SOHO space observatory sits in space between Earth and Sun and monitors the Sun continually.

The Sun's energy is generated by nuclear reactions in its core and makes its way to the surface over millions of years.

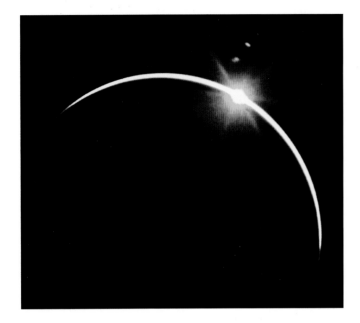

▲ *Every now and then, the Moon swings between the Sun and the Earth, blocking out the Sun and creating a shadow a few hundred miles wide on the Earth. This is called a solar eclipse. Sometimes, the Sun glints through a valley on the Moon's surface, as in this picture, creating an effect like a jewel on a ring.*

DATA: The Sun

- **DIAMETER**
  The Sun is a medium-siz star 865,000 miles across- 10 times the diameter of the Earth.

- **MASS**
  The Sun's weight is more than 300,000 times that of the weight of the Earth.

- **ENERGY CONSUMPTION**
  The Sun burns up 4 million tons of hydrogen fuel every second.

- **ENERGY PRODUCTION**
  The Sun's energy production each second could keep the USA supplied with electricity for 50 million years.

- **CORONAL TEMPERATURE**
  The temperature of the Sun's outer ring or corona is 2.7 million°F.

▶ *The heat from the Sun's core erupts on the surface in patches called granules. Here and there, giant flamelike tongues of hot hydrogen, called solar prominences, loop 60,000 miles out into space. Every now and then, too, huge five-minute eruptions of energy, called solar flares, burst from the surface. There are dark blotches on the Sun's surface, called sunspots, some fifty times the size of Africa. They are dark because they are slightly less hot than the rest of the surface. The number of spots seems to peak every 11 years, and some scientists believe these peaks are linked to spells of stormier weather on Earth.*

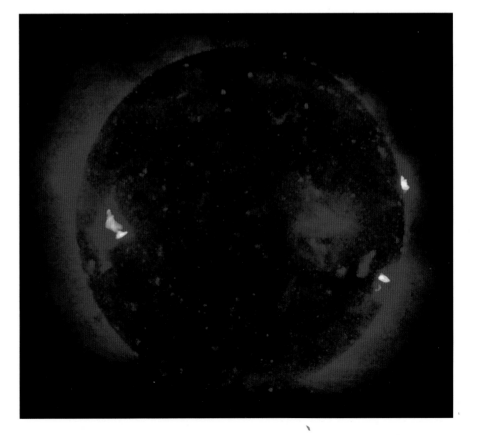

Inner planets

Mercury

THE INNER PLANETS are the four planets in the solar system that are nearest the Sun. Nearest the Sun is little Mercury, then comes Mars, Earth, and Venus. All four are made of rock, unlike the big planets farther out, which are made mainly of gas. Because they are made of rock, they have a hard surface, which a spaceship could land on, and they are sometimes called terrestrial (earthlike) planets. They all have an atmosphere of gas above the rocky surface-although Mercury's is very thin-but each is very different.

FACTS: About Mercury

◄ Mercury's atmosphere of sodium is so thin that there is nothing to stop meteors smashing into its surface—and nothing to smooth out any dents. So its surface is more deeply pitted with the scars of meteor impacts than the Moon's. All you'd see on a voyage across the surface would be vast empty basins, cliffs, and endless views of yellow dust.

• **Hot and cold**
Temperatures on Mercury veer from one extreme to the other because its atmosphere is too thin to provide any insulation. In the day, temperatures soar to 800°F, but at night they plunge to -300°F.

• **Mercury's brief year**
Mercury is so near the Sun that its orbit is very short. It gets round in just 88 days, compared with 365 days for Earth. On the other hand, it takes a long time to turn around—58.6 days. So its day lasts 58.6 Earth days.

• **Burning cold**
Mercury has small ice caps at each pole—but the ice is made from acid, not water.

DATA: The inner planets

MERCURY
• Mercury ranges from 28.5 million miles to 43.2 million miles from the Sun.
• Mercury's diameter is 3,024 miles and its mass is barely a twentieth of Earth's.

VENUS
• Venus is 66.6 million miles to 67.6 million miles from the Sun.

• Venus's diameter is 7,503 miles and its mass is about four-fifths that of Earth's.

MARS
• Mars is 141.3 million miles from the Sun.
• Mars's diameter is 4,207 miles and its mass is just over a tenth of Earth's.

FACTS: About Venus

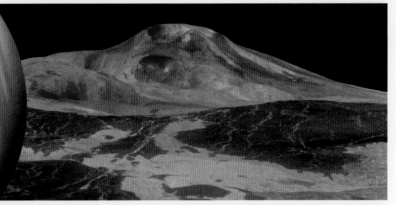

▲ *Venus is the hottest planet in the solar system, and its surface is as barren as any desert on Earth. The buildup of carbon dioxide gas in its atmosphere has created a runaway "greenhouse effect," trapping so much of the Sun's heat that temperatures reach a scorching 875°F (470°C).*

• **Evening star**
Venus reflects sunlight so well off its thick atmosphere that it shines like a star. But because it is quite close to the Sun, we can only see it in the evening just after the sun has gone down, which is why it is sometimes called the evening star. We can also see it just before sunrise.

• **Thick air**
Venus's atmosphere would be deadly to humans. It is very deep and thick, so pressure on the surface is enormous. It is also made mainly of poisonous carbon dioxide and filled with clouds of sulfuric acid gas belched out by the volcanoes on its surface.

FACTS: About Mars

• **High and deep**
Mars has the biggest volcano in the solar system, called Olympus Mons, 9 miles high, three times higher than Mt. Everest. It also has a canyon called Valles Marineris, which is 6,400 miles long and four times as deep as the Grand Canyon.

• **The red planet**
None of the space missions to Mars so far have found even the remotest trace of life. But in 1996, NASA scientists found what they though might be the fossil of a microscopic organism in a rock from Mars in the Arctic. So the search is on.

▶ *Mars is sometimes called the red planet because it is rusty red. The surface contains a high proportion of iron dust, and this has been oxidized (rusted) in its carbon dioxide-rich atmosphere. It has small ice caps.*

Giant planets

Saturn

OUT BEYOND MARS THERE are two planets far bigger than any others in the solar system. Jupiter and Saturn, the fifth and sixth planets out from the Sun, are gigantic. Jupiter is twice as heavy as all the other planets put together and 1,300 times as big as Earth. Saturn is not that much smaller. Unlike the inner planets, they are both made mostly of gas, and only their very core is rocky. This doesn't mean they are vast cloud balls. The huge pressure of gravity means the gas is squeezed until it becomes liquid or even solid.

FACTS: About Jupiter

◄ Jupiter's surface is covered in a thin layer of swirling clouds of ammonia, indicating powerful storms. One storm called the Great Red Spot is 25,000 miles across and has lasted at least 330 years.

• **Mighty magnet**
Jupiter's bulk and its fast spin churn up the metal insides of the planet so much that the planet becomes a giant dynamo creating a magnetic field ten times as strong as Earth's.

• **Many moons**
Jupiter has 16 moons. There are four big ones discovered by Galileo as long ago as 1610, which is why they are called the Galilean moons. Then there are 12 smaller ones.

Great Red Spot

Galilean moon

▼ The power of Jupiter's gravity drags volcanoes of sulfur from the surface of its moon Io.

• **Fast spinner**
Jupiter spins faster than any other planet. Despite its vast size, it turns right around in just 9.8 hours, so the surface is moving at 27,900 mph!

• **Hydrogen deeps**
Jupiter is made mostly of hydrogen and helium gas, but this is squeezed so hard by the planet's gravity that it turns to liquid. Beneath Jupiter's thin atmosphere of ammonia, there is an ocean of liquid hydrogen 15,500 miles deep.

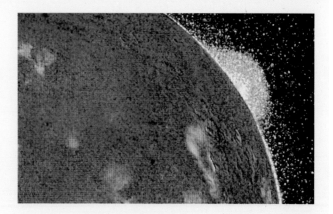

FACTS: About Saturn

▶ *Saturn is the most beautiful of all the planets, with its pale butterscotch surface of ammonia gases and its huge halo of rings.*

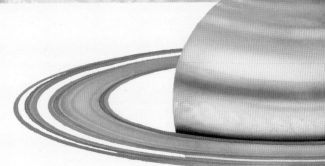

• Saturn's rings
Saturn's rings are countless billions of tiny chips of ice and dust. The rings are thin—no more than 160 feet deep—yet stretch 46,000 miles out into space.

▼ *Saturn's rings have definite bands, named with the letters A to G.*

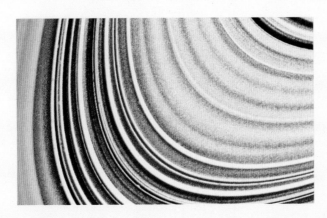

• Light planet
Saturn may be big, but it is surprisingly light, weighing 600 billion trillion tons. If you had a large enough bathtub, it would float.

• Most moons
Saturn has more moons than any other planet—at least 19. Iapetus is black on one side and white on the other. Enceladus is covered in shimmering balls of ice. Tethys was once almost split in half by a giant meteor, which left a giant crater. Titan is the only moon with an atmosphere.

• Windy planet
The surface winds on Saturn are faster than those on Jupiter, roaring around at 1,100 mph.

DATA: About the giant planets

JUPITER
- Jupiter ranges from 459.4 million miles to 505.7 million miles from the Sun.
- Jupiter's diameter is 88,650 miles and its mass is 318 times that of Earth's.
- It takes 11.86 years to orbit the Sun.
- Its surface temperature is -238°F.

SATURN
- Saturn ranges from 835 million miles to 934 million miles.
- Saturn's diameter is 74,732 miles and its mass is more than 95 times that of Earth's.
- It takes 29.46 years to orbit the Sun.
- Its surface temperature is -290°F.

Outer planets

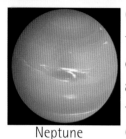

Neptune

OUT BEYOND SATURN are the seventh, eight, and ninth planets of the solar system: Uranus, Neptune, and Pluto, along with Pluto's companion Charon. Unlike the other planets, these were unknown to ancient astronomers. They are so far away and so faint that Uranus was only discovered in 1781, Neptune in 1846, Pluto in 1930, and Charon as recently as 1978. Uranus and Neptune are giant gas planets like Saturn and Jupiter. Pluto and Charon are rocky planets and may have been asteroids trapped by the Sun's gravity in the outer reaches of the solar system.

FACTS: About Uranus

- **Rollover planet**
  Unlike any of the other planets, Uranus does not spin at a slight angle. Instead it is tilted right over, and rolls around the Sun like a giant bowling ball. In summer, the Sun does not set for 20 years.

- **Blue planet**
  Uranus has an atmosphere of hydrogen and helium, but beneath that are oceans of liquid methane, and it is this that gives the planet its beautiful blue-green color.

◀ Uranus is so far from the Sun that temperatures drop to -340°F. Winds whistle through its atmosphere whipping up huge waves in the icy oceans of methane below.

FACTS: About Neptune

◀ Neptune has its own thin set of rings, like Saturn.

- **Blue planet**
  Like Uranus, Neptune has a thin atmosphere of hydrogen and helium, but is mostly deep oceans of liquid methane. The methane makes Neptune a beautiful cobalt blue.

- **Long year**
  Neptune is so far from the Sun that its orbit takes 164.79 years.

- **Discovering Neptune**
  Neptune's moon Triton is the only moon to orbit backward. It is the coldest place in the solar system -390°F and looks like a green melon with pink ice cream on the ends—ice caps of frozen nitrogen. Its volcanoes erupt ice.

DATA: The outer planets

URANUS
- Uranus ranges from 1.7 billion miles to 1.86 billion miles from the Sun.
- Uranus's diameter is 31,693 miles and its mass is over 14 times that of Earth's.

NEPTUNE
- Neptune ranges from 2.76 billion miles to 2.81 billion miles from the Sun.
- Neptune's diameter is 30,707 miles and its mass is over 17 times that of Earth's.

PLUTO
- Pluto ranges from 2.93 billion miles to 4.57 billion miles from the Sun.
- Pluto's diameter is 1,760 miles and its mass is just one-fiftieth of Earth's.

- **Discovering Neptune**
  Neptune was discovered because in the 1840s two young mathematicians, John Couch Adams in England and Urbain le Verrier in France, predicted where it should be from the way its gravity made a slight difference to Uranus's orbit. The planet was actually spotted by John Galle from the Berlin observatory on September 23, 1846.

  ▼ *This is a view of Neptune and its moon Triton taken by the Voyager space mission, which reached the planet in 1989.*

FACTS: About Pluto

▶ *Pluto and Charon are so far away from the Sun that the Sun looks little bigger in their sky than a star and shines as palely as the Moon on Earth. So surface temperatures plunge to -365°F (-220°C).*

- **Pluto**
  Pluto is very, very small, which is why it took so long to spot. Indeed, some people say it should not be called a planet at all. It is five times smaller than the Earth and 500 times lighter.

- **Charon**
  Pluto is only twice as big as its companion moon Charon. So they circle round each other locked in space like a pair of weight lifter's dumbbells. If you stood on Pluto's surface, you would see Charon in the sky, three times as big as our Moon, but never moving.

- **In and out**
  Pluto has an elliptical orbit that every now and then swings it closer to the Sun than Neptune.

Comets and meteorites

PLANETS AND MOONS are not the only things whirling around the Sun. Along with the Earth and its companions are thousands upon thousands of tiny bits and pieces of rock and ice of all shapes and sizes. Some are smaller than a car. Others are several hundred miles across. These lumps of space debris are called asteroids. Every now and then, a very large lump of debris swings in from the outer limits of the solar system, creating a comet in the night sky. And all the time, lumps of this debris cannon into the Earth as meteors, some penetrating right through to the ground as meteorites.

FACTS: About asteroids

- **The asteroid belt**
  Asteroids are little chunks of debris that never clumped together to make a planet when the solar system was young. There are probably a million or more lying in a belt circling the Sun between Mars and Jupiter.

- **Ceres**
  The first of the asteroids to be spotted—and the biggest—is Ceres, as big as Maine. The brightest is called Vesta, the only asteroid that can be seen with the naked eye.

- **The Trojan asteroids**
  The Trojans are two small groups of asteroids that circle the Sun on the same orbit as Jupiter.

▼ *Asteroids were first discovered in 1801, after a group of astronomers, calling themselves the Celestial Police, began hunting for a missing planet they were certain lay somewhere between Mars and Jupiter. Nowadays, new asteroids are discovered frequently. Each is given an identification number, and is named by the discoverer. Names vary from Greek goddesses to calculators.*

▲ *Every day, tons and tons of space debris rain down on the Earth, sometimes in such great concentrations that they make a golden rain in the night sky—called a meteor shower—as they hit the Earth's atmosphere and burn up. Meteors are space dust and lumps so small that they burn up long before they hit the ground. Meteorites are big enough to plunge right through the atmosphere and hit the ground. Most of these fall harmlessly into the oceans, and vary in size from lumps the size of shoes, to the meteorite the size of a car that hit Namibia, Africa, in 1920, creating an enormous crater.*

FACTS: About comets

▶ As it swings round the Sun, a comet's tail changes direction. It contains so little solid matter that it is blown out easily by the solar wind, the stream of charged particles flowing from the Sun— and so always points away from the Sun.

A tail of ionized atoms is blown out millions of miles behind the comet by the solar wind

At the heart of a comet is a tiny nucleus of dust and ice

• **Dirty snowballs**
Comets with their flaming tails are the most spectacular sights in the night sky. But they are actually just dirty balls of ice, only a few miles across.

• **Visitors from afar**
Many comets circle the Sun like the planets, but they have very long, stretched out orbits, and spend most of their time in the far reaches of the solar system. We see them only when their orbit brings them, for a few weeks, close to the Sun.

• **Glowing tails**
The comet's tail is created as the comet hurtles towards the Sun and begins to melt. A vast plume of gas, millions of miles across, is blown out behind it by the solar wind, and this is what we see shining in the night as it catches the sunlight.

• **Periodics**
Some comets, called Periodics, appear at regular intervals. Encke's comet comes every 1,206 days. Halley's Comet comes every 76 years.

• **Speeding comets**
Comets speed up as they near the Sun, sometimes reaching speeds of up 1.2 million mph (2 million km/h). But far away from the Sun they slow down to speeds of little more than 600 mph, which is why they stay away for so long.

▲ Halley's comet, discovered by Edmund Halley (1656-1742), appeared before the Battle of Hastings in 1066, and some say it was the star of Bethlehem.

Stars

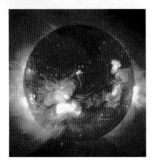

A star in close-up:
our Sun

THE FEW THOUSAND STARS you see twinkling in the night sky are just a tiny fraction of the trillions scattered through the Universe. Like our Sun, they are huge fiery balls of hot gas. They shine because they are burning. Deep inside, atoms of gas fuse together in nuclear reactions that boost temperatures to millions of degrees, making their surfaces glow. A star goes on glowing, sending out light, heat, radio waves, and radiation, until its nuclear fuel–mainly hydrogen gas–is used up.

FACTS: About giants and dwarfs

- **Giant stars**
  Most stars are much the same size as our Sun— about 800,000 miles across. But some are giants 100 times as big, or supergiants some 300 times as big.

- **Dwarf stars**
  Dwarf stars are actually very small—smaller than the Earth. Very old stars can shrink under the power of their own gravity to even tinier neutron stars—no bigger than a major city, but so dense that they are as heavy as the Sun!

- **Starlight**
  The color of starlight tells us what the star is made of, and how hot it is.

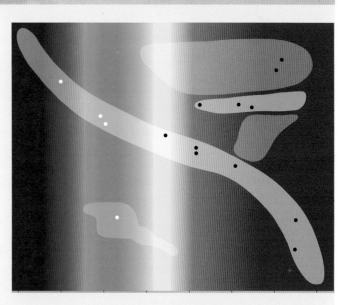

▲ *The color of a star depends on how bright it is. The Herzsprung-Russell diagram shows how the hotter and whiter stars glow, the brighter they are; the redder and cooler they glow, the dimmer they are. All medium-size stars behave like this and form a band, called the Main Sequence stars, across the middle of the graph. Giants, dwarfs, and neutron stars fall outside this band.*

◀ *Stars vary in brightness or "magnitude." The Herzsprung-Russell diagram shows how we expect stars of a certain color to be a certain brightness, their Absolute Magnitude. But if a star is far away, it looks dimmer than expected. This is its Relative Magnitude.*

▲ Stars are being born and dying all over the Universe. The bigger the star, the shorter its life. The biggest stars end their lives in gigantic explosions called "supernovas," which are, briefly, the brightest things in the night sky as incredibly hot gas billows away.

FACTS: About constellations

• **Patterns in the stars**
Ancient astronomers found their way around the heavens by looking for patterns of stars in the night sky. These patterns are called constellations. Astronomers now identify 88 of them, such as the Great Bear and Orion.

• **The Big Dipper**
The Big Dipper, also known as the Great Bear or Ursa Major, is one of the best known constellations in the northern sky. It points toward the Pole Star, indicating north.

• **Alpha and beta**
The stars in each constellation are named after letters in the Greek alphabet. The brightest star in each constellation is called Alpha, the next brightest Beta, and so on. So Alpha Pegasi is the brightest star in Pegasus, the Flying Horse.

DATA: Stars

• **THE BRIGHTEST-LOOKING STAR**
Sirius, the Dog Star, is the brightest star in the night sky. But it is quite nearby (8.6 light-years) so its brightness is only relative.

• **THE BRIGHTEST STAR**
Deneb burns as bright as 60,000 Suns, but because it is 1,800 light-years away, it looks dimmer than Sirius.

• **THE BIGGEST STAR**
No one knows what the biggest star is, but Antares is very big, 700 times as big as our Sun.

• **STARS WITH PLANETS LIKE THE SUN**
At least nine other stars, including 51 Pegasi, are now known to have planets, like our Sun has.

▲ Without constellations to help us, it would be hard to locate stars in the sky, but there is no real link between the stars in a constellation—they are completely imaginary patterns.

Galaxies and nebulae

OUR SUN IS JUST ONE OF A MASSIVE collection of two billion stars arranged in a shape like a spinning fried egg. This gigantic collection of stars is called the Galaxy. It gets its name from the Greek for "milky", because we see it as a milky white band across the night sky–called the Milky Way. But the Galaxy is just one of many millions of similar giant groups of stars, also called galaxies (with a small "g"), scattered throughout the Universe.

▲ On a clear night, fuzzy patches of light can be seen among the stars. Some of these patches are distant galaxies. But others are huge clouds of dust called nebulae, many times bigger than any star. Only a few, called glowing nebulae, actually glow themselves; most are bright because the dust reflects starlight, just as clouds on Earth reflect sunlight. This picture show the famous Horsehead nebulae in the constellation of Orion, so-called because it is shaped a little like a horse's head.

FACTS: About galaxies

▶ Spiral galaxies are spinning, Catherine wheel-shaped galaxies, such as the Milky Way and Andromeda galaxies. They have a dense core of stars, surrounded by long whirling arms.

▶ Barred spiral galaxies are variations on spiral galaxies with a central bar from which arms of stars trail like water from a spinning garden sprinkler.

▶ Elliptical galaxies are huge egg-shaped galaxies sometimes containing a trillion stars. They are the oldest galaxies of all, some over 12 billion years old.

▶ Irregular galaxies are different from the others in that they have no obvious shape at all, and may have formed from the debris of colliding galaxies.

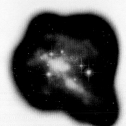

Stars start life in giant clouds of dust and gas called nebulae. Stars are born in these clouds as gravity pulls the dust into clumps—so ferociously that the pressure makes them glow.

• **Visible galaxies**
Only three galaxies apart from the Milky Way can be seen with naked eye: the Large and Small Magellanic Clouds and the Andromeda galaxy.

• **Far lights**
Galaxies contain many millions of stars, each as big as our Sun. But they are so far away that even with a reasonably good telescope, most look like blurs in the night sky. Andromeda, one of the nearest galaxies beyond the Milky Way, is more than 3 million light-years away!

• **The size of galaxies**
Galaxies are absolutely gigantic. Although they contain millions or even trillions of stars, they are mostly empty space, for the stars are far apart. If each star was a person, the nearest neighbor would be almost as far away as the Moon.

• **How many galaxies?**
Astronomers estimate that there are something like 20 trillion galaxies in the Universe.

• **Spiral galaxies**
Just as the planets spin around the Sun, so spiral galaxies seem to be spinning too, which is why they have trailing arms.

• **Groups**
Galaxies are often clustered in Groups of 30 or more. The Milky Way is part of the Local Group.

The band of stars across the night sky called the Milky Way is an edge-on view of our own Galaxy, a vast cluster of stars 100,000 light-years across. It is a spiral galaxy, and our Sun is just one of millions of stars on one of the trailing arms. As it whirls round, it sweeps the Sun (and with it the Earth) in a huge circle 60 million miles every hour. The Sun travels more than 100,000 light-years to go around once—and it will get round in 200 million years. So the dinosaurs had just appeared on Earth last time it was where it is now.

The Milky Way is 100,000 light-years across and 1,000 light-years thick.

Black holes

GRAVITY IS THE FORCE that holds the Universe together. It is the force that keeps the Earth in one piece, keeps us on the ground, and keeps planets circling the Sun and the stars together in galaxies. Yet it can also be so powerfully destructive that it can squeeze stars to nothing and suck galaxies into oblivion. When some giant stars burn out, there is nothing to hold them up, and they start to collapse under the force of their own gravity. As they shrink, they get denser and denser, and their gravity becomes even stronger... and so they get denser and denser, and their gravity becomes stronger still. Eventually, they shrink to nothing...and if one goes on shrinking, it may create a hole in space, called a black hole.

FACTS: About gravity and orbits

- **Orbits**
  Things stay in orbit when their forward momentum exactly balances the pull of gravity.

- **Earth's orbit**
  Earth stays on the same path around the Sun because it is bowling through space too fast to be drawn in by the pull of the Sun—yet not so fast that it can overcome the Sun's pull altogether and hurtle off into space.

- **Satellites**
  Satellites seem to hang in space because they are moving too fast to fall into the Earth.

Launched too slow, the satellite falls back to Earth

Launched too fast, the satellite hurtles off into space

Launched at the right speed, the satellite goes into orbit

◁ A satellite has to be launched at exactly the right speed and on exactly the right trajectory (path) to be placed successfully in orbit. The lower the orbit is to be, the faster it must go if it is to avoid being pulled down by gravity. For an orbit 23,000 miles above the ground, the satellite has to be going fast enough to complete an orbit in exactly 24 hours—the same time it takes the Earth to spin. So a satellite placed in this orbit stays in the same place above the Earth.

◁ The destructive power of gravity can be seen on Jupiter's moon Io. The giant planet Jupiter is so massive that its gravity alternately pulls and sucks so powerfully on Io as it revolves that the insides of the moon get incredibly hot—so hot that volcanoes burst onto the surface.

FACTS: About the search for black holes

• **Do black holes exist?**
No one has ever seen a black hole. Indeed, we cannot be sure they actually exist. But the bright radiation from quasars (see below)—and from the center of our galaxy may be signs that black holes do exist.

• **Where are black holes found?**
Some scientists think there is a giant black hole at the center of each spiral galaxy. Some believe there are tiny ones everywhere.

◁ *This bright galaxy may have a black core.*

As matter is sucked into the hole, it is ripped apart and jets of radiation are sent out

Matter whirls around the black hole like water around a plug hole

◁ *Black holes are places where gravity is so strong that it sucks everything in, even light. This is why they are called black holes. They form when a star or galaxy collapses to the stage where it is so dense that its gravity sucks it all into an impossibly small point called a singularity. Gravity around the singularity is so ferociously powerful that it not only sucks in light, but even bends space and time. The brightest objects in the Universe, called quasars, may be like the screams of mangled stars—the intense radiation from matter being ripped to shreds as it is sucked into a black hole.*

How far to the stars?

THE UNIVERSE IS VERY, VERY BIG and the distances between the stars are so huge that astronomers don't measure them in miles or kilometers, but in light-years–which is how far light travels in a year. Light is the fastest thing in the Universe and travels at about 186,000 miles per second, so a light-year is 5.86 billion miles. The nearest star is 4.3 light-years away. The most distant objects so far discovered are more than 13 billion light years away. That means that light takes more than 13 billion years to reach us–so astronomers are looking at them as they were 13 billion years ago!

DATA: Distances in space

- **THE NEAREST PLANET**
  The nearest planet to Earth is Venus, which is more than 24 million miles away.

- **THE FURTHEST PLANET**
  The farthest planet from Earth in the solar system is Pluto, which is nearly 3.7 billion miles away.

- **THE NEAREST STAR**
  The nearest star is Proxima Centauri, in the constellation of the Centaur, which is 4.3 light-years away.

- **THE NEAREST OUTSIDE GALAXY**
  The nearest galaxy outside our own is the Andromeda galaxy, which is some 2.5 million light-years away.

- **THE FURTHEST GALAXY**
  The farthest galaxy–a quasar–yet seen is more than 13 billion light-years away across the Universe.

- **DISTANCE TO THE MOON**
  The Moon varies from 220,274 miles to 252,152 miles from Earth.

- **DISTANCE TO THE SUN**
  The Sun is between 91 million miles and 94 million miles away.

- **PARSECS**
  Astronomers may measure large distances in parsecs. A parsec is 3.26 light-years. Parsec distances are worked out by using the geometry of "parallaxes"–the way a star seems to shift slightly in position in the night sky as the Earth moves around the Sun.

Distances in
space are vast

◀ *The distance to the Moon is measured to within a few yards by bouncing laser beams off mirrors left on the Moon by astronauts.*

FACTS: Galactic distances

- **Standard candles**
  To find the distance of a nearby galaxy, astronomers look for stars within it whose brightness they are sure of. These include stars called "cepheid variables," "supergiant stars," and giant exploding stars called "supernova."

- **Very distant galaxies**
  Astronomers cannot pick out individual stars in very distant galaxies, so they estimate the distance by tricks, such as the Tully-Fisher technique, based on how it appears to be spinning. The faster it spins, the brighter it should be. So if it is dim, it must be far away.

- **Red shift**
  The redder a distant galaxy looks, the faster it is moving away from us.

▶ *The distance to the Sun and nearby planets is measured by bouncing radar beams off them. Space probes help with planets farther away.*

▶ *Distances to the nearer stars are generally worked out either by the parallax method (see parsecs) or by estimating their brightness. Astronomers can guess how bright a star should look compared to other stars from its color. If it actually looks brighter than it should, it must be nearby; if it looks dimmer, it must be farther away.*

▼ *Distances to the galaxies are worked out by looking for "standard candles," stars whose brightness we can be sure of. Really far off galaxies call for even more ingenious methods.*

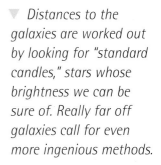

Working out distances

The method astronomers use to work out the distance of an object in space depends on how far away it is. For nearby objects, such as the Sun and the planets, they can use radar beams, and estimates can be accurate within a few thousand miles. They measure distances to nearby stars by gauging their brightness, and estimates are accurate only to within a few billion miles. Distances to far galaxies are accurate only to within a few billion light-years!

Space travel

THE AGE OF SPACE EXPLORATION began in 1957, when powerful rocket engines boosted the Russian satellite *Sputnik 1* free of Earth's gravity. This was the start of an extraordinary series of adventures for mankind which has seen scores of satellites put in space, man's first steps on the Moon, live broadcasts from Mars, and space probes venturing past the outer planets of the solar system. These probes have not only beamed back the first pictures of new previously unknown moons but have also provided remarkable insights into the nature of the Universe.

FACTS: About spacecraft

- **Rocket power**
  Very powerful rockets are needed to push a spacecraft clear of Earth's gravity—but once clear, such power is no longer needed. So rockets are made in separate stages, each of which falls away when its fuel is spent.

- **The space shuttle**
  In the early days, manned spacecraft could only be used once, with just a tiny capsule holding the astronauts falling back to Earth at the end of the mission. The US space shuttle was the first spacecraft that could be reused, landing back on Earth like an airplane. The boosters that launch it into space are recovered.

- **Space probes**
  Unmanned space probes, guided by computer, have now visited all the planets but Pluto, the smallest and most distant, and probes have actually landed on Mars and Venus. Late in 1997, the Mars Pathfinder beamed back live pictures from the surface of Mars.

- **Slingshot effect**
  Space probes voyaging to the planets use gravity to help them travel huge distances on very little fuel. As they pass each planet, their gravity pulls them in and hurls them onward on a slightly different course, like a slingshot.

▲ *The space shuttle is launched with solid fuel booster rockets that fall away but are then recovered. Typical shuttle missions include launching and repairing satellites and performing scientific experiments.*

FACTS: About satellites and probes

- **Staying in orbit**
  Satellites stay in space because they are circling, or "orbiting," the Earth just too fast to be pulled down by Earth's gravity—but not so fast that they fly off into space.

- **Staying still**
  An orbit 22,000 miles above the ground takes exactly 24 hours—the same time it takes the Earth to spin once. So satellites on this orbit stay in exactly the same place above the Earth. This is called a geostationary orbit.

- **Hubble Space Telescope**
  Satellites not only give a clear view of the Earth from space, but a better view of space too, because they are free from Earth's atmosphere. The Hubble Space Telescope, launched in 1990, gives extraordinary pictures of distant objects in space.

▲ *Spacecraft can be remarkably ungainly looking objects. Once they are free of the Earth's atmosphere, there is no need for streamlining, and aerials and dishes stick out in all directions. This is the Galileo launched in 1989 to explore Jupiter.*

DATA: Milestones in Space Exploration

- **THE FIRST LIVING CREATURE IN SPACE**
  Laika the dog was launched in the Russian *Sputnik 2* in November 1957. Sadly she could not be brought back.

- **THE FIRST MAN IN SPACE**
  The first man in space was the Russian cosmonaut Yuri Gagarin, in April 1961.

- **THE FIRST SPACE WALK**
  In 1965, Russian cosmonaut Alexei Leonov was the first man to walk in space.

- **THE FIRST MEN ON THE MOON**
  The American *Apollo* astronauts Neil Armstrong and Buzz Aldrin stepped on the Moon on July 21, 1969.

- **REACHING VENUS**
  In 1970, the Soviet Union's *Venera 7* landed on Venus.

- **PASSING SATURN**
  In 1969, the US *Pioneer 11* probe reached Saturn and discovered new moons.

- **REACHING NEPTUNE**
  In 1989, the US *Voyager 2* reached the planet Neptune.

- **MARS LANDING**
  In 1997, the Mars Pathfinder roved the surface of Mars, beaming back pictures.

History of the Universe

THE UNIVERSE PROBABLY BEGAN about 13 billion years ago. One moment there was nothing. The next there was a minute, unimaginably hot ball—and suddenly the Universe burst into existence with the biggest explosion of all time, called the Big Bang, swelling at a totally astonishing rate. This explosion was so big that everything is still hurtling away from it, which is why the Universe is expanding. Even now, 13 billion years on, astronomers can detect the faint afterglow, called the cosmic microwave background radiation, spread throughout the night sky.

FACTS: Expanding universe

- **Receding galaxies**
  As astronomers observe space, they can see galaxies zooming away from us in all directions at astonishing speeds. The farther they are away, the faster they seem to be moving. This can only mean the Universe is expanding.

- **The Big Crunch?**
  Some scientists think the Universe will go on expanding forever. This is called the "open universe" idea. Others think gravity will put a break on its expansion. If there is a great deal of dark matter—matter we can't detect—it may be enough to make it all start to shrink again. Then it may end in a Big Crunch.

▶ *We know how fast galaxies are receding because of the color of light from them. The faster they are receding, the more light waves from them get stretched out. When light waves are stretched they look redder. This is called red shift. The redder the light, the faster the galaxy is moving away.*

FACTS: About how the solar system was born

- **Swirling cloud**
The solar system did not exist 4.6 billion years ago. There was just a hot, dark cloud of gases swirling around the Sun. The planets began to form as the cloud cooled and droplets began to clump together.

- **The birth of the Earth**
The Earth probably formed as gravity began to pull together clumps of star dust from around the Sun. But this early Earth was a molten ball.

▼ *No one knows where the material that formed the solar system came from. Some think it was the remnants of an exploded star, others the result of a collision between stars.*

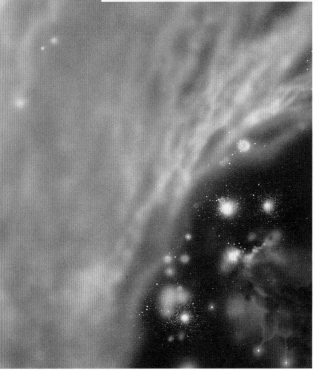

◄ *Scientists have worked out how the Universe began by mathematical calculations and experiments with huge machines called particle accelerators, which hurl atoms together. It started with a tiny hot ball, which cooled to many billions of degrees as it grew to the size of a football. In a split second, it swelled to create a space bigger than a galaxy in a period called inflation. Within this space, all the matter and energy and forces began to take the form we know in the Universe today. At first, it was a dense chaotic soup of particles and energy. But then atoms began to form, and the atoms formed clouds, and the clouds galaxies.*

Key facts: The Universe

The planets

Planet	Diameter (miles)	Av. distance from Sun (million miles)	Rotation period	Length of year	Tilt of axis	Mass, if Earth =1	Brightness
Mercury	3,031	35.98	58.65 days	87.97 days	2°	0.055	-1.9
Venus	7,520	67.2	243.01 days	224.7 days	177.3°	0.815	-4.4
Earth	7,926	93	23.93 hours	365.26 days	23.45°	1	
Mars	4,217	141.6	24.62 hours	686.98 days	25.19°	0.107	-2.0
Jupiter	88,849	483.6	9.84 hours	11.86 years	3.1°	317.94	-2.7
Saturn	74,900	886	10.23 hours	29.46 years	26.7°	95.18	+0.7
Uranus	31,764	1,784	17.9 hours	84.01 years	98°	14.53	+5.5
Neptune	30,776	2,794	19.2 hours	164.79 years	29.6°	17.14	+7.8
Pluto	1,429	3675	6.39 hours	248.54 years	122.5°	0.002	+15.1

Milestones

- AD 140: Ptolemy devises his model of the motion of the planets and stars.
- 1543: Nicolaus Copernicus shows that the planets revolve around the Sun, not the Earth.
- 1610: Galileo uses a telescope to see things, such as the phases of Venus and the Moons of Jupiter.
- 1659: Christiaan Huygens discovers the rings of Saturn.
- 1781: William Herschel discovers the planet Uranus.
- 1801: Giuseppi Piazzi discovers Ceres, the first asteroid.
- 1846: John Galle discovers the planet Neptune.
- 1929: Edwin Hubble shows that there are other galaxies beyond our own and that the Universe is expanding.
- 1930: Clyde Tombaugh discovers the planet Pluto.
- 1978: James Christy finds Pluto's moon Charon.
- 1995: Michael Mayer and Didier Queloz spot a planet circling the star 51 Pegasi.

The Constellations

Andromeda
Antlia, the Air Pump
Apus, the Bird of Paradise
Aquarius, the Water Bearer
Aquila, the Eagle
Ara, the Altar
Aries, the Ram
Auriga, the Charioteer
Boötes, the Herdsman
Caelum, the Graving Tool
Camelopardalis, the Giraffe
Cancer, the Crab
Canes Venatici, the Hunting
Dogs
Canis Major, the Great Dog
Canis Minor, the Little Dog
Capricornus, the Sea Goat
Carina, the Keel
Cassiopeia
Centaurus, the Centaur
Cepheus
Cetus, the Whale
Chamaeleon, the Chameleon
Circinus, the Compasses
Columba, the Dove
Coma Berenices, Berenice's
Hair
Corona Australis, Southern
Crown
Corona Borealis, the Northern
Crown
Corvus, the Crow
Crater, the Cup
Crux, the Southern Cross
Cygnus, the Swan
Delphinius, the Dolphin
Dorado, the Swordfish
Draco, the Dragon
Equuleus, the Foal

Eridanus
Fornax, the Furnace
Gemini, the Twins
Grus. the Crane
Hercules
Horologium, the Clock
Hydra, the Water Snake
Hydrus, the Little Snake
Indus, the Indian
Lacerta, the Lizard
Leo, the Lion
Leo Minor, the Little Lion
Lepus, the Hair
Libra, the Scales of Justice
Lupus, the Wolf
Lynx, the Lynx
Lyra, the Lyre
Mensa, the Table
Microscopium, the Microscope
Monoceros, the Unicorn
Musca, the Fly
Norma, the Rule
Octans, the Octant
Ophiuchus, the Serpent Bearer
Orion
Pavo, the Peacock
Pegasus, the Flying Horse
Perseus

Phoenix, the Phoenix
Pictor, the Painter
Pisces, the Fishes
Piscis Austrinus, the Southern
Fish
Puppis, the Poop
Pyxis, the Compass
Reticulum, the Net
Sagitta, the Arrow
Sagittarius, the Archer
Scorpius, the Scorpion
Sculptor, the Sculptor
Scutum, the Shield
Serpens, the Serpent
Sextans, the Sextant
Taurus, the Bull
Telescopium, the Telescope
Triangulum, the Triangle
Triangulum Australe, the
Southern Triangle
Tucana, the Toucan
Ursa Major, the Great Bear
Ursa Minor, the Little Bear
Vela, the Sails
Virgo, the Virgin
Volans, the Flying Fish
Vulpecula, the Fox

Key facts: The Universe

Planets' moons

Earth's moon
- The Moon

Mars's moons
- Phobos
- Deimos

Jupiter's moons
- Metis
- Adastrea
- Amalthea
- Thebe
- Io
- Europa
- Ganymede
- Callisto
- Leda
- Himalia
- Lysithea
- Elara
- Ananke
- Carme

- Pasiphae
- Sinope
- Phoebe

Saturn's moons
- Unnamed
- Pan
- Atlas
- Prometheus
- Pandora
- Janus
- Epimetheus
- Mimas
- Enceladus
- Tethys
- Telesto
- Calypso
- Dione
- Helene
- Rhea
- Titan

- Hyperion
- Iapetus
- Phoebe

Uranus's moons
- Cordelia
- Ophelia
- Bianca
- Cressida
- Desdemona
- Juliet
- Portia
- Rosalind
- Belinda
- Puck
- Ariel
- Umbriel
- Titania
- Oberon

Neptune's moons
- Naiad
- Thalassa
- Despina
- Galatea
- Larissa
- Proteus
- Triton
- Neraid

Pluto's moon
- Charon

Saturn, with 19 moons, has more moons than any other planet in our Solar System.

Nearest and brightest stars

Nearest stars
- Sun (0.0 light-years away from Earth)
- Proxima Centauri (4.2)
- Alpha Centauri A (4.3)
- Alpha Centauri B (4.3)
- Barnard's star (5.9)
- Wolf 359 (7.6)
- Lalance 21185 (8.1)
- Sirius A (8.6)
- Sirius B (8.6)
- UV Ceti A (8.9)

Brightest stars
- Sun (0.0-light years away from Earth)
- Sirius A (8.6)
- Canopus (200)
- Alpha Centauri (4.3)

- Arcturus (36)
- Vega (26)
- Capella (42)
- Rigel (910)
- Procyon (11)
- Achernar (85)

Space exploration

- **1926** The American engineer Robert Goddard designed and launched the first liquid fuel rocket.
- **1942** Wernher von Braun developed the V2 rocket in Nazi Germany.
- **1957** The world's first artificial satellite, the USSR's *Sputnik 1*, was launched.
- **1957** The Russian dog Laika became the first living creature in space aboard *Sputnik 2*.
- **1961** The Soviet cosmonaut Yuri Gagarin became the first man in space aboard *Vostok 1*.
- **1963** The Soviet cosmonaut Valentina Tereshkova became the first woman in space.
- **1966** The USSR's unmanned probe *Lunar 9* landed on the Moon.
- **1969** US astronauts Neil Armstrong and Edwin Aldrin were the first men to walk on the Moon.
- **1972** *Apollo 17* was the sixth and last US manned mission to the Moon.
- **1973** First US space station *Skylab* launched.

- **1980** The US *Voyager 1* took the first detailed photos of Saturn's ring systems and discovered six additional moons.
- **1981** The US space shuttle *Columbia*, the world's first reusable spacecraft, was launched.
- **1982** The Soviet probe *Venera 13* sent back color photos of the surface of Venus.
- **1986** The shuttle program was halted for several years after the shuttle *Challenger* exploded, killing its crew of seven.
- **1990** The Hubble space telescope was launched.
- **1996** US scientists found evidence in meteor fragments that microbes may have existed on Mars.

Quiz: The Universe

1. The Earth is 24,815 miles round at the equator: true or false?

2. There is water on the Moon: true or false?

3. The footprints left by the astronauts on the Moon in the 1960s are still there: true or false?

4. How big are the smallest sunspots–as big as Africa or 50 times as big as Africa?

5. On what is the SOHO space telescope targeted?

6. A light-year is the distance light travels in a year: true or false?

7. Who was the first man in space?

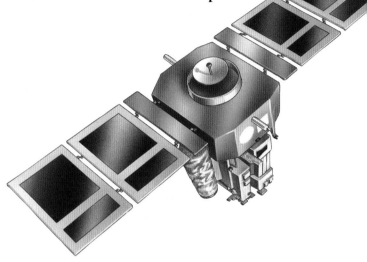

8. What did Neil Armstrong say when he stepped onto the Moon?

9. How many manned missions to the Moon were there–six or 22?

10. Who was the first man to walk in space?

11. What is the launch path of a satellite called?

12. What is the name of the space probe that landed on Mars in 1997?

13. Mercury has ice caps of acid: true or false?

14. Which planet is closest to Earth?

15. Which of the planets in the Solar System has the shortest year?

16. Are there volcanoes on Venus?

17. Which planet is furthest from the Sun?

18. Saturn would float if you could find a bath big enough: true or false?

19. The surface of Jupiter is spinning at 27,900 mph: true or false?

20. Comets are made mostly of ice: true or false?

Answers:

1. True

2. True

3. True

4. 50 times as big as Africa

5. The Sun

6. True

7. Yuri Gagarin in 1961

8. "That's one small step for man, one giant leap for mankind."

9. Six

10. Alexei Leonov in 1965

11. Its trajectory

12. Mars Pathfinder

13. True

14. Venus

15. Mercury (88 days)

16. Yes

17. Pluto

18. True

19. True

20. True

PLANET EARTH

Home planet

THE EARTH MAY SEEM QUITE STILL but it is actually spinning around like a top at more than 500 miles per hour-faster than most jet planes. It is also hurtling through the dark on its orbit around the Sun at over 60,000 miles per hour! Every year it covers 582,729,560 miles in its orbit around the Sun. The Earth's entire journey around the Sun takes exactly 365.242 days, which is why there are 365 days in our year. We make up the extra 0.242 days in our calendar by an extra day every fourth year, called a leap year-then miss out a leap three centuries out of four.

FACTS: About latitude and longitude

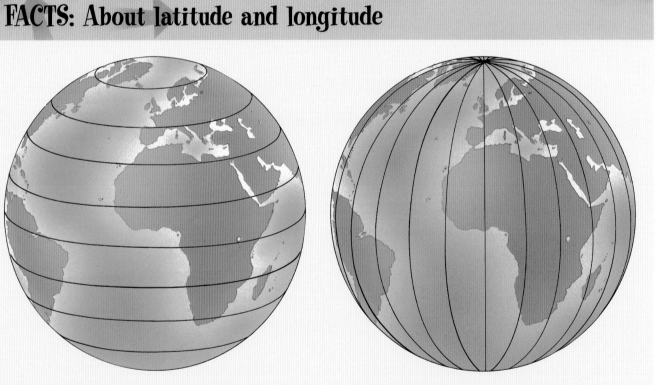

▲ Lines of latitude are called parallels because they form rings around the Earth parallel to the equator, which is latitude 0°. The North Pole is latitude 90°N.

▲ Lines of longitude, or meridians, run around the Earth from pole to pole, dividing the world up like the segments of an orange.

• **Lines of latitude**
Every place on the Earth's surface can be pinpointed by two figures: its latitude and longitude. Lines of equal latitude (called parallels) form rings around the Earth parallel to the equator. A place's latitude is given in degrees North or South of the equator.

• **Lines of longitude**
Lines of longitude (called meridians) run around the Earth from North to South. A place's longitude is given as degrees West or East of the Prime Meridian, which runs through Greenwich in London, England.

In spring, north and south get equal sun

When the north is tilted away from the Sun, it is winter here, but summer in the south

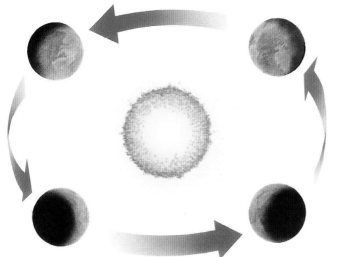

When the north is tilted toward the Sun, it is summer here, but winter in the south

In fall, north and south get equal sun

▲ *We get seasons because the Earth is always tilted over in the same direction. So when the Earth is on one side of the Sun, the northern hemisphere (the world north of the equator) is tilted toward the Sun, bringing summer here. At this time, the southern hemisphere is tilted away, and so gets winter. When the Earth is on the other side of the Sun, the northern hemisphere is tilted away, bringing winter, while the south gets summer.*

DATA: Our Home Planet

- **DISTANCE OF THE EARTH FROM THE SUN**
  The Earth is 92.7 million from the Sun. At its nearest, it is 91,200,636 miles away. At its furthest it is 94,300,884 miles away.

- **SPIN TIME**
  The Earth spins round once every 23 hours, 56 mins and 4.09 seconds. The Sun appears to comes back to the same place in the sky once every 24 hours.

FACTS: About the time of day

- **Time zones**
  As the Earth spins, the Sun is always rising in one place and setting in another. So the time of day varies around the world. When it's dawn where you live, it's sunset on the other side of the world. To make it easier to set clocks, the world is split into 24 time zones, one for each hour of the day. As you go east around the world, you put clocks forward by one hour for each zone—until you reach a line called the International Date Line. If you carry on across the Date line, you carry on adding hours, but put the calendar a day back.

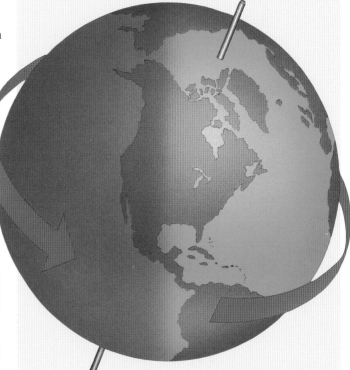

▲ *Half the world is facing the Sun and is brightly lit; the other half is facing away and in darkness. As the Earth spins around on its axis, the dark and sunlit halves move around, bringing day and night around the world. Because the Earth is turning eastward, the Sun appears from the ground to come up in the east and sink again in the west. The Earth turns once every 24 hours, which is why days are 24 hours long.*

Earth's atmosphere

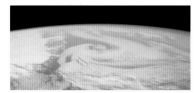

WRAPPED AROUND the Earth is a thin blanket of gases called the atmosphere. This blanket is no thicker on the Earth than the peel on an apple. Yet without it, the Earth would be as lifeless as the Moon. It gives us the air we need to breathe. It gives us clean water to drink. And it keeps us warm by trapping the Sun's heat-yet at the same time shielding us from the most harmful of its rays. It gives us weather, too, for everything we call weather is the churning of the atmosphere's lowest layer, next to the ground, as it is stirred by the Sun's warmth.

FACTS: About water in the air

- **Water cycle**
  All the water on Earth is forever being recycled in a process called the water cycle (see below).

- **Watery planet**
  Over 70 percent of the Earth's surface is covered by water. At any one time, just one percent is in the atmosphere, 97 percent is in the oceans. The rest is in lakes and rivers or frozen as ice.

- **Humidity**
  The air is full of invisible water vapor. The amount of water vapor in the air at any one time is known as its humidity.

- **Relative humidity**
  The total amount of moisture in the air is its "absolute" humidity. But the warmer air is, the more water it can hold, so meteorologists look at "relative" humidity, or rh, which is the percentage of moisture actually in the air relative to the maximum it could hold at that temperature.

- **Turning to water**
  As air cools, its rh must go up, because cool air can hold less moisture. Eventually, the rh reaches 100 percent and the vapor condenses into drops of water. This is called the dew point.

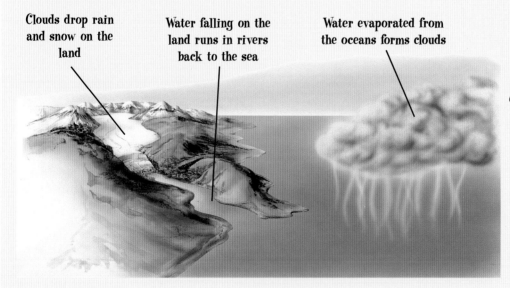

Clouds drop rain and snow on the land

Water falling on the land runs in rivers back to the sea

Water evaporated from the oceans forms clouds

◄ *The Sun's heat makes water evaporate from the oceans and rise into the air. As it rises, it cools off and condenses into tiny drops of water, forming clouds. When the drops get big enough, they fall as rain or snow back into the oceans—or onto the land where the water runs in rivers back to the sea.*

The atmosphere all looks like thin air, but scientists have shown that it has five or more layers or "spheres," each with its own characteristics. We live in the lowest layer, called the troposphere. This layer is just 7 miles thick, but 75 percent of the atmosphere's gases sink into this layer. As you go higher and higher, the gases get more and more spread out until by the time you are about 600 miles up, the gases are so thin or "rarefied" that the atmosphere fades off into space.

FACTS: About air pressure

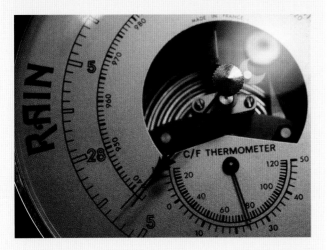

⚠ Air pressure can be measured on a device called a barometer. Barometers help tell you if a storm is on its way, because storms are linked to low pressure. If the pressure drops sharply, you can be sure rain and wind are on their way.

- **Atmospheric pressure**
  At sea level, the atmosphere is so dense that there is a crush of air molecules. This crush creates enormous pressure in the air, called atmospheric or air pressure.

- **Wind and pressure**
  Air pressure varies from time to time and place to place. High pressure pushes air toward zones of low pressure, and this is what creates winds—air moving from high pressure to low pressure zones. The sharper the pressure difference, the stronger the wind.

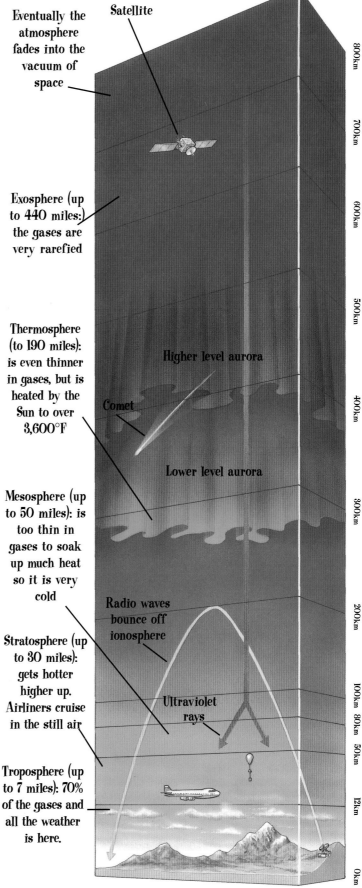

Satellite

Eventually the atmosphere fades into the vacuum of space

Exosphere (up to 440 miles): the gases are very rarefied

Thermosphere (to 190 miles): is even thinner in gases, but is heated by the Sun to over 3,600°F

Higher level aurora

Comet

Lower level aurora

Mesosphere (up to 50 miles): is too thin in gases to soak up much heat so it is very cold

Radio waves bounce off ionosphere

Stratosphere (up to 30 miles): gets hotter higher up. Airliners cruise in the still air

Ultraviolet rays

Troposphere (up to 7 miles): 70% of the gases and all the weather is here.

800km
700km
600km
500km
400km
300km
200km
100km
80km
50km
12km
0km

Weather

THERE ARE MANY DIFFERENT KINDS OF WEATHER-rain, snow, sun, wind, fog, mist, frost. But all of them are simply changes in the air caused by the varying effect of the Sun's warmth. Winds blow up, for instance, when the Sun heats some places more than others, setting the air moving. Rain falls when air warmed by the Sun lifts moisture high enough for it to form big drops of water when it condenses. Frost and snow occur when the power of the Sun is reduced. All weather comes down to three factors: the way the air moves (wind), its moisture content (humidity), and its temperature (warmth).

FACTS: About thunderstorms

• **Thunder clouds**
Huge thunderclouds are built up by strong updrafts on a hot day or along a cold front. Eddies in the cloud hurl water drops and ice together so hard they become charged with static electricity (see p151). Positive particles clustering at the top of the cloud and negative particles at the bottom, create a charge difference. Soon the charge difference builds up so much that lightning flashes from positive to negative.

▼ *Fork lightning flashes from cloud to ground. Sheet lightning flashes within the cloud. Lightning heats the air so much it bursts in a clap of thunder.*

Fronts
The stormiest weather in many places is linked to depressions (low pressure regions). A wedge of warm air intrudes into the heart of depressions, and the worst weather occurs along the edges of this wedge, called fronts, where the warm air meets the cold. As the depression moves over, the fronts bring a distinct sequence of weather.

Cold front

▲ *Once the warm front has passed, the weather becomes milder and clearer for a while. But after a few hours, a buildup of thunderclouds and gusts of wind warn that the trailing edge of the wedge, called the cold front, is on its way. As the cold front passes over, the thunderclouds unleash short but heavy rain showers, and even thunderstorms, before calm returns.*

FACTS: About clouds and rain

- **Making clouds**
  Clouds form when water vapor rises with warm air then condenses as the air cools in the upper air. It rains when the water drops in clouds get too heavy to float on the air.

- **Icy rain**
  Most rain comes from water droplets freezing into ice particles in a cloud. The particles grow into snowflakes, then melt into raindrops as they fall—or stay as snow if the air is cold.

- **Tropical rain**
  In the tropics, raindrops form inside tall clouds as small raindrops join up to make bigger drops heavy enough to fall as rain.

◀ *Rain clouds are gray because they are so thick with large drops of water that they block out the sunlight.*

▼ *Natural snowflakes are six-sided and consist of crystals that are mostly flat plates, but can be needles or columns. But under a magnifying glass, you can see that no two snowflakes are ever the same.*

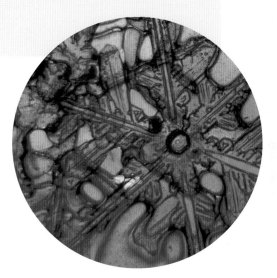

Warm front

▲ *First to arrive is the leading edge of the wedge of warm air, or warm front, where warm air slides over cold air. As it rises it forms banks of clouds along the front. So the coming of the warm front is heralded by feathery "cirrus" clouds high in the sky. Soon the clouds thicken until the sky is full of slate-grey "nimbostratus" clouds, which bring long periods of steady rain.*

DATA: Weather

- **WETTEST**
  The wettest place in the world is Tutunendo in Colombia which gets 460 inches of rain anually—18 times as much as New York.

- **THE COLDEST AND HOTTEST**
  The coldest place is Vostok in Antarctica, where it averages -72°F. The hottest is Dallol in Ethiopia, where it averages 93°F in the shade, and can get much hotter.

153

Wind

ALL WIND IS SIMPLY AIR MOVING. Strong winds are air moving fast. Gentle breezes are air moving slowly. Air moves because the Sun warms some places more than others, creating differences in air pressure which push the air about. Warmth makes the air expand and rise, lowering air pressure. But where the air is cold and heavy, air pressure is high. Winds blow from areas where pressure is high, called anticyclones, to areas where pressure is low, called cyclones or depressions. The greater the difference in pressure, the stronger the wind is.

FACTS: About hurricanes

◁ *Every summer, nine or so hurricanes develop in the eastern Atlantic and spiral westward to the Gulf of Mexico, tracked all the way by satellite. Here a hurricane's distinctive spiral of clouds is seen hitting the coast of Texas.*

▷ *Hurricanes are shape like huge spiral cakes. Winds spiraling in towards the low pressure center, or eye, help line the thunderclouds into great walls of cloud towering into the sky.*

• **Hurricanes and typhoons**
Hurricanes are the Atlantic version of the cyclone storms that batter eastern coasts in the tropics. In the Pacific, they are known as typhoons.

• **What a hurricane does**
When a hurricane strikes, trees can be ripped up and buildings flattened by winds gusting up to 220 mph. Vast areas can be battered and swamped by torrential rain, and coasts can be overwhelmed by the "storm surge"—the mound of seawater that builds up in the storm center.

• **Hurricane year**
There are on average 103 typhoons and other tropical storms and 45 hurricanes every year.

• **How hurricanes start**
Hurricanes begin in the eastern Atlantic as thunderstorms set off by moist air rising over the warm ocean. If the water is warm enough, they pile up together, then begin to spiral westward across the ocean, growing bigger all the time.

• **Gaining power**
By the time the hurricane has crossed the Atlantic, it is spiraling tighter round its center or "eye." The eye shrinks to just 30 miles across and winds howl round it at over 70 mph.

FACTS: About tornadoes

• Twisters

Tornadoes are tiny spirals of wind that sweep past in less than 15 minutes—but 180 mph winds and a low pressure center that sucks like a giant vacuum cleaner can toss people, cars, and buildings high in the air like toys. They are common from March to July in "Tornado Alley" in the Midwest.

• Supercells

Tornadoes are set off by giant thunderclouds called supercells. Winds whipping through the clouds set updrafts spinning. As they spin, they create a vortex, which hangs from the cloud base down to the ground, like an elephant's trunk.

▲ *Often it is the torrential rain and the storm surge of ocean water that do most of the damage in a hurricane, but the ferocious winds can also wreak havoc, blowing down trees and buildings.*

• The eye

The air in the dead center or eye of the hurricane is at very low pressure and is very calm. As the eye passes over, the winds may drop altogether and a small circle of blue sky may often be seen. But the lull is short-lived, for the rain and wind are at their strongest either side of the eye.

• Big wind

A hurricane can be 500 miles across, and it can take 18 hours to pass over.

• Hurricane warning.

Each hurricane is given a name and tracked by satellite to help give people plenty of warning that one is on its way.

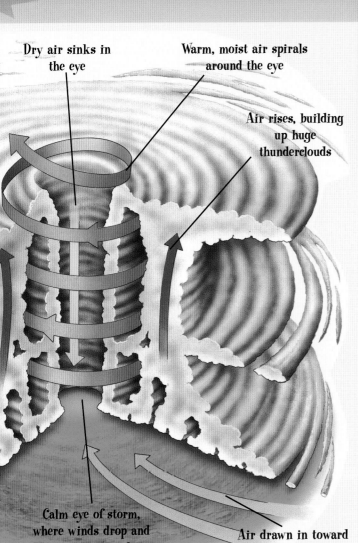

Dry air sinks in the eye

Warm, moist air spirals around the eye

Air rises, building up huge thunderclouds

Calm eye of storm, where winds drop and pressure is very low

Air drawn in toward the low pressure at the center of the storm

Structure of the Earth

THE EARTH IS NOT QUITE THE SOLID BALL it seems. Using sensitive equipment to detect the pattern of vibrations from earthquakes and big explosions, scientists have shown it has quite a complicated structure. Only a very thin shell, called the crust, is completely solid. Inside are a number of different layers, some solid, but some soft like molasses, while some of the core is molten metal. Atomic reactions in the core mean the Earth gets hotter and hotter as you go deeper toward the center, reaching over 12,600°F in the center—hotter than the surface of the Sun.

FACTS: Inside the Earth

- **Thin crust**
  The Earth's crust of rock is on average 25 miles thick under the continents and just 3.5 miles beneath the oceans.

- **Soft mantle**
  Beneath the crust is the mantle, nearly 2,000 miles thick and made of rock so warm it flows like molasses, only very slowly.

- **Metal core**
  In the center of the Earth is a core of metal (iron with a little nickel). The outer core is so hot it is molten. The inner core is even hotter, but pressures are so great the metal stays solid.

- **Crust edge**
  The boundary between the crust and mantle is called the Mohorovicic discontinuity.

- **Rigid top**
  The very top of the mantle is stiff and attached to the crust, so that they move as one—so scientists sometimes talk of the "lithosphere," which is the crust and the outer 60 miles of the mantle.

- **Soft underneath**
  Beneath the lithosphere in the upper mantle is the softer "asthenosphere" down to 120 miles, where rock circulates very slowly.

▲ *The world is a bit like a partly boiled egg, with a hard shell or crust, a white of semisoft rock called the mantle, and a yolk or core of molten and solid metal.*

- **Lower down**
  Below the asthenosphere is a third, stiffer layer within the upper mantle, called the mesosphere.

- **Mesophere**
  Heat makes the whole of the mantle churn very slowly, over millions of years. Sometimes big hot blobs rise right up from the core to the crust. These "superplumes" may create huge volcanoes.

▲ The pulling apart of tectonic plates creates giant cracks in the Earth's surface. Usually, these cracks are hidden underwater on the ocean bed. But in Iceland, the crack that runs right down the middle of the Atlantic ocean bed comes to the surface. Each side of this valley is a different plate, and they are slowly pulling apart.

▼ The giant plates that make up the Earth's hard shell, or lithosphere, are always moving, although very, very slowly. In some places, plates are crunching together, and one of the plates—typically a continent—rides over the other and forces it down into the Earth's interior. This process is called subduction. In other places— usually in mid-ocean on the seabed—plates are pulling apart. But even as they pull apart, so they gain new material as hot molten rock wells up through the gap and solidifies on the exposed edges. This is called mid-ocean spreading.

FACTS: Moving plates

- **Tectonic plates**
  The Earth's rocky crust is broken into 20 or so huge fragments called tectonic plates. As these move slowly about, they set off earthquakes and volcanoes, and pile up mountain ranges.

- **Continental drift**
  As tectonic plates move, they carry the continents slowly about the world.

▼ The Earth's crust consists of 20 or so plates which carry continents as they move. Africa and South America were once joined. Europe is drifting slowly farther from America.

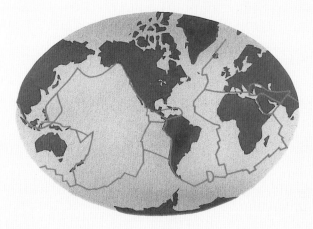

In the middle of the ocean, where plates are pulling apart, new molten rock wells up to create a series of ridges under the sea

Deep trench in the ocean where a plate is subducted

Ocean

Subducted plate pushed into the Earth's interior

In "subduction zones," plates are pushing together, pushing one plate beneath the other

Rock from the melting plate burns up to erupt through as volcanoes

Continent

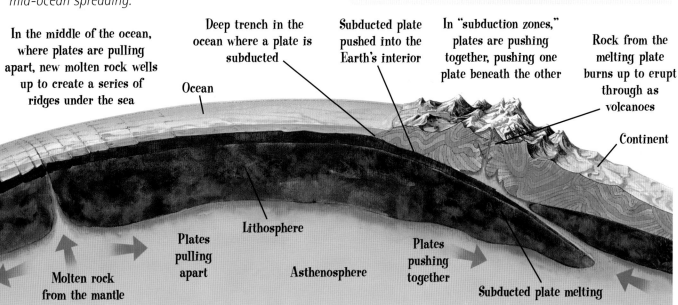

Lithosphere

Plates pulling apart

Molten rock from the mantle

Asthenosphere

Plates pushing together

Subducted plate melting

History of the Earth

THE EARTH probably formed about 4.6 billion years ago from debris spinning around the Sun. At first, it was a molten ball, but it gradually cooled and a thin crust formed around the outside. The first signs of life—probably bacteria—appeared nearly four billion years ago. But the first animals with shells and bones easily preserved as fossils did not appear until less than 600 million years ago. It is mainly with the help of such fossils that geologists have built up a picture of Earth's history since then. Very little is known about the four billion years before this, called Precambrian time.

Earth formed 4.55 billion years ago

Archean 4,600-2,500 million years ago (m.y.a.)

▲ This spiral shows some events in Earth's history, starting with its origin at the center of the spiral and the coming of humans at the end. The scale is distorted because so little is known about what happened in the first 85 percent of Earth's history—so the last 15 percent is given much more space. If Earth's history were crammed into a day, humans would appear only at the end, just two seconds before midnight.

FACTS: Geological time

- **Units of time**
  Just as the day is divided into hours, minutes, and seconds, so geologists divide the Earth's history into time periods. The longest are Eons, billions of years long; the shortest are Chrons, a few thousand years long. In between come Eras, Periods, Epochs, and Ages.

- **Fossil time**
  Because different plants and animals lived at different times in Earth's past, geologists can tell how long ago rocks formed from the fossils in them. Using fossils, they have divided the Earth's history since Precambrian times into 11 periods.

- **Geological column**
  Layers of rock form one on top of the other, so the oldest is usually at the bottom, unless they have been disturbed. The sequence of layers from top to bottom is called the geological column.

FACTS: About dating

- **Fossil dating**
  By looking for certain key fossils, geologists can tell whether one layer of rock is older than another so they can then place it within the geological column. This is called "biostratigraphy".

- **Absolute date**
  Fossils can only show if a rock is older or younger, not give a date in years—and many rocks don't contain fossils. To give an "absolute" date, geologists often use radioactivity.

- **Radioactive dating**
  After certain substances, such as uranium and rubidium, form, their atoms slowly break down into different atoms, sending out rays as they do so. The rays are called radioactivity. By assessing how many atoms in a rock have changed, geologists can tell how old it is.

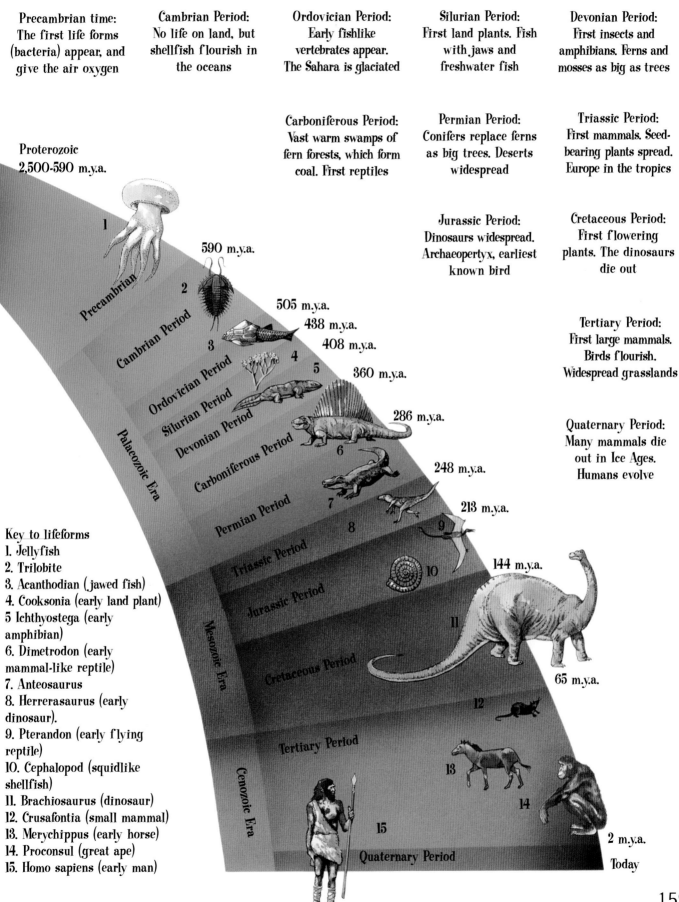

Precambrian time: The first life forms (bacteria) appear, and give the air oxygen

Cambrian Period: No life on land, but shellfish flourish in the oceans

Ordovician Period: Early fishlike vertebrates appear. The Sahara is glaciated

Silurian Period: First land plants. Fish with jaws and freshwater fish

Devonian Period: First insects and amphibians. Ferns and mosses as big as trees

Carboniferous Period: Vast warm swamps of fern forests, which form coal. First reptiles

Permian Period: Conifers replace ferns as big trees. Deserts widespread

Triassic Period: First mammals. Seed-bearing plants spread. Europe in the tropics

Jurassic Period: Dinosaurs widespread. Archaeopertyx, earliest known bird

Cretaceous Period: First flowering plants. The dinosaurs die out

Tertiary Period: First large mammals. Birds flourish. Widespread grasslands

Quaternary Period: Many mammals die out in Ice Ages. Humans evolve

Proterozoic 2,500-590 m.y.a.

590 m.y.a.

505 m.y.a.

438 m.y.a.

408 m.y.a.

360 m.y.a.

286 m.y.a.

248 m.y.a.

213 m.y.a.

144 m.y.a.

65 m.y.a.

2 m.y.a.

Today

Precambrian

Cambrian Period

Ordovician Period

Silurian Period

Devonian Period

Carboniferous Period

Permian Period

Triassic Period

Jurassic Period

Cretaceous Period

Tertiary Period

Quaternary Period

Palaeozoic Era

Mesozoic Era

Cenozoic Era

Key to lifeforms
1. Jellyfish
2. Trilobite
3. Acanthodian (jawed fish)
4. Cooksonia (early land plant)
5. Ichthyostega (early amphibian)
6. Dimetrodon (early mammal-like reptile)
7. Anteosaurus
8. Herrerasaurus (early dinosaur).
9. Pterandon (early flying reptile)
10. Cephalopod (squidlike shellfish)
11. Brachiosaurus (dinosaur)
12. Crusafontia (small mammal)
13. Merychippus (early horse)
14. Proconsul (great ape)
15. Homo sapiens (early man)

159

Rocks

ROCKS ARE THE HARD MASS the ground is made of. You can only see bare rock exposed on the surface in a few places–cliffs, mountain crags, and quarries. But it is there everywhere, not far beneath the city streets or the thin covering of soil or vegetation. Some rocks are just a few million years old; some are almost as old as the Earth. But they all tend to be very tough solids made of tiny crystals or "grains" of naturally occurring chemicals called minerals. All these minerals came originally from the Earth's hot interior, but at the surface they form three kinds of rock: igneous, sedimentary, and metamorphic.

FACTS: About igneous, sedimentary, and metamorphic rock

▲ Igneous rocks, such as this granite, make up 90 percent of the Earth's crust. Granite is an intrusive rock and formed underground.

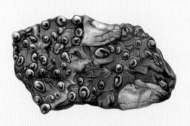

▲ Although most surface rock is igneous, 75 percent of the land surface is covered by thin layers of sedimentary rock, such as this limestone.

▲ Metamorphic rock, such as this hornfels, is rock made when other rock is altered by extreme heat or pressure.

- **Igneous rock**
  Igneous rock is formed from red hot magma (molten rock) that wells up from the Earth's interior. Some erupts on the surface through volcanoes and cools to form "volcanic" or "extrusive" igneous rock. Some is pushed up under the surface, forming "intrusive" igneous rock.

- **Acid and basic igneous rock**
  There are many different kinds of rock. Some, such as granite, are light in color and are made from acidic magma (rich in silica). Others, such as basalt, are darker and made from basic magma.

- **Sedimentary rock**
  Sedimentary rock forms in thin layers from debris that settles mainly on the seabed and is then squeezed and cemented over millions of years into solid rocks. Some, such as limestone, are made mainly from plant and animal remains. Most are made from fragments of rock worn away by the weather.

- **Metamorphic rock**
  Metamorphic rock is made when other rocks are crushed by movements of the Earth's crust or scorched by magma—and changed so much that they form a new kind of rock, such as marble or slate.

160

FACTS: About coal and oil

▼ *In the Carboniferous Period, there were huge tropical swamps filled with giant, treelike ferns. It is these that most coal formed from, as the remains of the plants were buried and squeezed.*

1. Remains of swamp plants were first buried and squeezed to make peat

2. As they became buried deeper, heat and pressure changed the peat to brown coal

3. Further pressure changed brown coal to black bituminous coal and finally anthracite

- **Fossil fuels**
  Coal, oil, and natural gas are fossil fuels, which means they formed over millions of years from the remains of plants and small creatures.

- **Carboniferous swamps**
  Most coal formed from the remains of plants that grew in huge, warm swamps in the Carboniferous Period, 300 million years ago.

- **Oil bearing rocks**
  Oil formed from the remains of tiny plants and animals that lived in warm seas. As they died, they were buried and squeezed into oil, then collected in porous (spongelike) layers of rock.

- **Crude oil**
  Oil usually comes up from the ground as thick, black "crude" oil and must be refined for use.

▼ *The materials rocks are made of is continually recycled to make new rocks in a process called the rock cycle. Magma from the interior cools to form igneous rock, which is gradually worn away by the weather. The fragments are washed down into the sea and settle on the seabed to form sedimentary rock. Both sedimentary and igneous rock may be altered into metamorphic rock—and all three are eventually broken down so that they too can be formed into new sedimentary rocks.*

1. Igneous rocks form from magma forced up from the Earth's interior

2. Weather wears away the rock and fragments are washed into the sea, then settle on the seabed

3. Sediments buried under the seabed are cemented into layers of rock, then lifted up above the sea to be worn away again

161

Minerals

MINERALS ARE THE natural chemicals from which the Earth's crust is made. A few are powdery or resinous, but most are crystals. Usually, minerals occur as a mass of tiny crystals or grains. Occasionally, crystals grow as big as flagpoles. Geologists identify minerals by various factors including the color and shape of the crystal. There are 2,000 or so different minerals, but fewer than a hundred are common. A handful of minerals are pure chemical elements that occur naturally, such as gold or silver. Most are compounds, of which by far the most common are silicates.

FACTS: Gems

- **Gems**
  Gems are especially rare and beautiful mineral crystals such as rubies and emeralds.

- **Veins and geodes**
  Many precious gems form either in veins, where hot volcanic fluid forces its way into a crack in the rock, or in gas pockets in cooling volcanic rock, called geodes.

  ▲ *Gems are rare because they only form naturally under very special conditions—usually deep within volcanic rocks. A few can now be made artificially, but these are not so precious.*

- **Diamonds**
  Diamonds are very hard, very rare—and very old. They were probably made by the mighty collision of continents during subduction (see page 157) and taken deep into the Earth. They are only found because volcanoes bring them near the surface again after billions of years.

- **Colored gems**
  Many gems get their vivid colors from tiny traces of chemicals within them. Traces of iron turn common clear quartz into purple amethyst. Manganese turns quartz pink.

FACTS: About crystals

- **What are crystals**
  Crystals are glassy-looking, brittle solids that form in regular shapes, with sharp corners and flat sides.

- **Crystal shapes**
  Crystals are regular and there are only a certain number of possible basic regular shapes, called systems—cubic, pyramid, and so on. The crystals of each mineral fit into one of these systems.

▶ *Minerals only rarely form in large, distinct crystals like these. Most of the time they form much smaller grains, and are mixed in with other minerals in rocks. Granite, for instance, is made of the minerals feldspar, quartz, and mica, along with small amounts of other minerals. Quartz is a silicate mineral—the most common silicate mineral of all—but over 99 percent of it is actually mixed in with other minerals in granite and other rocks, such as sandstone.*

Twists of silver

Bismuth rarely occurs in pure form in nature. It is usually mixed with sulfur

Silver rarely looks silvery in nature because exposure to air tarnishes the surface black

FACTS: Elements & silicates

- Native elements
  Native elements are minerals that occur naturally as pure chemical elements, including all those shown on this page.

- Silicates
  Silicates are minerals that form when the chemical elements silicon and oxygen—two of the most common elements on Earth—combine with a metal. There are over 500 of them, including quartz, olivine, and pyroxene.

▼ *Gold is rare but almost always found in pure form because it just won't mix with any other mineral.*

Copper only rarely occurs in pure form. Normally it is linked into minerals, such as chalcopyrite

Yellow fluorite is a rare mineral made of calcium and fluorine

The green crystals are uraninite, chemically uranium oxide, the main source of the metal uranium

Yellow crystals of sulfur are often found around the smoking vents of volcanoes

Volcanoes

VOLCANOES ARE PLACES where hot molten rock or "magma" from the Earth's interior erupts on the surface. With some volcanoes, it oozes out gently and flows overground as lava—red hot liquid rock. Others get clogged up with thick plugs of magma and then suddenly burst through in a mighty explosion that sends up jets of steam and hurls scorching fragments of debris from under the plugs thousands of feet in the air. Most volcanoes occur near the cracks between the giant tectonic plates that make up the Earth's surface (page 157), but a few occur at "hot spots" where plumes of hot magma rise under the crust.

FACTS: Types of volcanoes

- **Thick and thin magma**
  Volcanoes take many forms, but the most explosive volcanoes occur near subduction zones where the collision of tectonic plates creates a very thick, sticky "acid" magma that clogs up the volcano easily. Where plates are pulling apart, the magma is less acid and runs freely.

- **Cinder volcanoes**
  Most volcanoes are made of solidified lava, but some are mounds of ash.

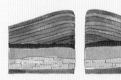

◁ *When the lava is quite runny, it floods out far and wide, creating a broad, gently sloping "shield" volcano.*

◁ *The thick lava from explosive volcanoes piles up steeply around the volcano, creating a cone.*

◁ *In "strato" volcanoes, alternate layers of ash and lava build up as ash falls on the lava flow from each eruption.*

▶ *The biggest eruptions are powered by a combination of steam and bubbles of carbon dioxide gas. Extreme pressure normally keeps them dissolved in the magma, but as the eruption begins the pressure drops and bubbles begin to form in the magma and swell rapidly. The eruption sends out three kinds of material apart from steam and gas—clouds of ash, solid fragments of the volcanic plug called tephra or volcanic bombs, and lava. Sometimes, lethal clouds of glowing ash hurtle down the slope.*

▽ *It is very hard to tell exactly when a volcano is going to erupt. But vulcanologists can get an idea by keeping a very careful watch on the slopes of the volcano, using laser rangefinders for accuracy. Any very slight change in slope might be the magma bulging up underneath, indicating an imminent eruption.*

Eruptions begin with a build up in pressure in the "magma chamber" beneath the volcano

▲ *Water heated under pressure underground by hot magma can burst onto the surface in a ferocious jet of steam and hot water called a geyser. The biggest geysers are hundreds of feet high.*

Big eruptions can send so much ash into the upper air that they blot out the sun and turns the world cool

Tephra vary in size from tiny "lapilli" to volcanic "bombs," which can measure up to 3 feet across

Lava flows look spectacular, but it is ash that is really deadly

FACTS: Famous eruptions

▲ *The eruption of Mt. St. Helens in Washington state in 1980 was one of the biggest to rock North America this century. The eruption blew away the top of the mountain and blanketed the forest far around with ash.*

- **Big bang**
  The eruption of Krakatoa, near Java, in 1883, was so loud that people heard it in North America.

- **Gray skies**
  The eruption of Mt. Tambora in Java, in 1815, sent up so much dust that the sun was blocked out right around the globe, causing two years of poor summers.

- **Roman remains**
  When Mt. Vesuvius in Italy erupted in AD 79, the people of the Roman town of Pompeii were buried instantly. The remains of the city, almost perfectly preserved under the ash, were discovered in the 18th century.

- **Biggest in human history**
  There was a giant eruption 20,000 years ago of Sumatra's Mt. Toba, which covered the entire island in ash 1,000 feet deep.

- **Biggest ever**
  One of the biggest-ever eruptions covered nearly all of India in lava 65 million years ago.

Earthquakes

EVEN A PASSING TRUCK can make the ground tremble, but most earthquakes are the ground shuddering as the huge tectonic plates that make up the Earth's surface (see page 157) grind past each other. Most of the time the plates slide past each other quietly. But they sometimes jam. Then pressure builds up until they suddenly lurch on again, sending shock waves radiating in all directions. The nearer a place is to where the earthquake began—called the epicenter on the surface—the more severe the earthquake is. The worst earthquakes can bring down mountains and destroy cities.

FACTS: Earthquake zones

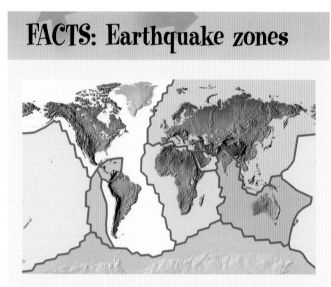

▲ Earthquake zones—places that suffer earthquakes repeatedly—are near plate edges, such as SE Europe and the Pacific coast.

• San Andreas
The San Andreas fault in California is where two great plates slide past each other, often setting off earthquakes, such as the one that destroyed San Francisco in 1906.

• Predicting earthquakes
Earthquakes are hard to predict, but they are most likely to occur in earthquake zones—especially when there has not been one for some time. Seismologists use satellites and laser beams to detect slight movements, and look for changes in the magnetism of rocks.

DATA: The worst earthquakes

- **856**: 200,000 people killed in Damghan, Iran.
- **1138**: 230,000 people killed in Aleppo, Syria.
- **1556**: 830,000 people killed in Shansi, China.
- **1737**: 300,000 people killed in Calcutta, India.
- **1908**: 100,000 people killed in Messina, Italy.
- **1920**: 200,000 people killed in Gansu, China.
- **1923**: 144,000 people killed in Kwanto, Japan.
- **1976**: 255,000 people killed in Tangshan, China.
- **1995**: The earthquake in Kobe, Japan, killed 5,200 people, destroyed 190,000 buildings, and left 300,000 people homeless.
- **1999**: 40,000 people killed in northwestern Turkey
- **2004**: 225,000 people killed in 12 Asian countries
- **2005**: 80,000 people killed in Pakistan

Raised freeways are very vulnerable to earthquake damage

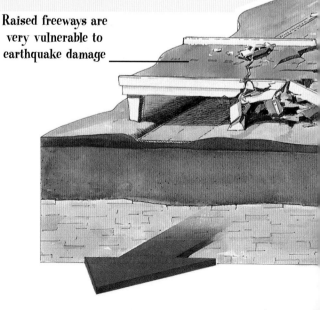

FACTS: About earthquake measurement

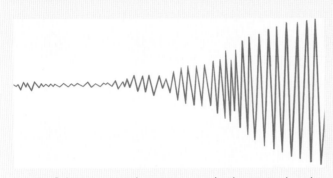

▲ *Seismometers detect tremors in the ground and display them on a seismograph. The strong vibrations of big earthquakes show as dramatic zigzags.*

- **Richter scale**
  The severity of an earthquake, measured on a machine called a seismometer, is usually assessed on the Richter scale, which goes from 1 (slight tremor) to over 9 (severe earthquake).

- **Mercalli scale**
  The Richter scale gives the absolute magnitude (size) of an earthquake, but no idea of its effects. These are sometimes assessed on the Mercalli scale, which rates the damage done on a scale of 1 (barely noticeable) to 12 (total destruction).

Earthquakes usually last only a few minutes, but their effects can be devastating

Tall buildings are especially prone to earthquake damage

▼ *This picture shows the destruction that occurs when buildings lie directly over a fault in the Earth's crust. But the shock waves—called seismic waves—can be devastating even tens of miles from the epicenter. A great deal of damage is done by an earthquake itself, as the tremors shake buildings to pieces and snap roadways. But they can also fracture gas pipes and electricity cables and set off terrible fires.*

This earthquake is set off by the two edges of a fault sliding past each other

Mountains

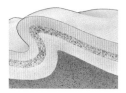

MOUNTAINS LOOK FAIRLY PERMANENT but they are continually being created and destroyed. Most of the biggest mountains are actually quite young in geological terms. The Himalayas of Asia, for instance, include the world's highest peaks, yet they were first raised less than 40 million years ago—and they are still growing today. Mountains are created in one of a number of ways. Most are created by the folding of rock layers as the huge tectonic plates that make up the Earth's surface crunch together. Others are created as crustal movements lift up huge blocks. Others are created by volcanic eruptions.

FACTS: About fold mountains

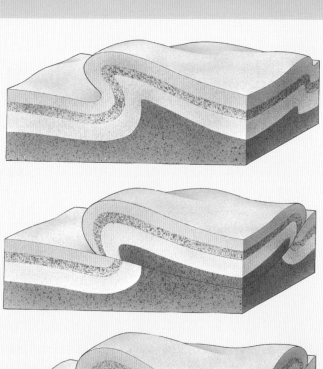

- **Fold ranges**
  Most of the world's greatest mountain ranges—the Himalayas, the Andes, the Rockies, the Caucasus, and the Alps—are created by the crumpling edges of colliding tectonic plates. This is why they often form long narrow ranges along the edges of continents. The Himalayas were created by the collision of India with Asia.

- **Runny mountains**
  The rock in mountains is not completely rigid. It flows a bit like very stiff molasses. So ranges, such as the Himalayas, are flowing out and getting flatter at the edges, at the same time as they are being pushed up.

- **Dip and strike**
  The angle at which folded rock layers are tilted is the "dip." This can be anything from a few degrees to over 90°. The direction of the fold is the "strike."

- **Upfold and downfold**
  Downfolds (like a dish) are called synclines; upfolds (like an arch) are called anticlines.

- **Overturned folds**
  Sometimes a fold may fold right over. This is called an "overturned" fold. If it folds so far that it rests on the next fold it is said to be "recumbent."

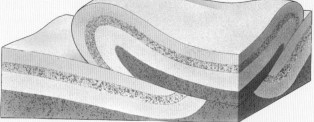

▲ If tectonic plates go on pushing together, the folding may go well beyond a simple fold (top). First it overturns and the layers begin to snap (middle). Finally the layers snap altogether, creating a "nappe."

The Alps were created by folding, but the dramatic shape of the Matterhorn, one of the highest Alpine peaks was created by glaciers.

DATA: The highest mountains

- The world: Everest in the Himalayas 29,021 feet.
- South America: Aconcagua 22,829 feet.
- North America: Mt. McKinley 20,320 feet.
- Africa: Kilimanjaro 19,336 feet.
- Europe: El'brus in Russia 18,506 feet.
- Australasia: Papua New Guinea's Mt. Wilhelm 16,020 feet.

FACTS: Faults & blocks

As the tectonic plates of the Earth's crust jostle together, they may put rocks under such strain that they fracture, creating cracks or "faults" in the rock. Large blocks of rock may then be thrown up to create mountains.

- **Where faults occur**
  Faults occur mainly in areas that are called "fault zones." These lie mostly along the edges of tectonic plates.

- **Normal fault**
  In most faults, the cracking of the Earth's crust as tectonic plates pull apart allows a block of rock to slip straight down. In a "wrench" fault, however, blocks slip sideways past each other. In a "reverse" fault, one block slides up over another as plates crunch together.

- **Horsts and rifts**
  If a block of rock is thrown down between two faults it may create a deep, steep-sided "rift" valley. If the block is thrown upward, it creates a high plateau called a horst.

A fault scarp is a cliff, exposed as a massive block of rock is thrown up or down

No mountain range lasts forever. Sooner or later they are worn down by the weather. Frost, for instance, may shatter rocks on mountain peaks, leaving the lower slopes littered with fragments known as scree.

Rivers

RIVERS RUN DOWN to the sea or lakes wherever there is enough rain or melting snow to keep them flowing. Even when it is not raining, most rivers in moist regions are kept flowing by water from underground. This is because a lot of rain does not flow directly over the land, but seeps into the ground–only to bubble up lower down, in places called springs. Most rivers are very tiny as they start high up in the hills, tumbling over rocks and rapids. But they get bigger further down as they are joined by tributaries (side rivers). As they near the sea, they run in broad, smooth-flowing curves called meanders.

Heavy rainfall and melting snow high up starts a river with plenty of water

High up, the river tumbles over rocks and rapids in steep, narrow valleys

FACTS: About river valleys

◁ The Grand Canyon in Arizona is one of the world's deepest river valleys, carved by the Colorado River over millions of years. The area is so dry that there is little rain to wear away the valley sides, so these sides are often steep cliffs.

• **River power**
Rivers continually batter their banks and beds with running water, sand, and pebbles. Over thousands of years, rivers can carve huge valleys out of solid rock.

• **Valley to plain**
To start with, river valleys are narrow, steep-sided, and winding—and they are usually like this near their source in the hills. But, with time, they carve out broader, flatter valleys, and they meander over a wide "floodplain"—a flat area liable to flooding when heavy rain or melting snow makes the river full.

▲ *Every river has a natural tendency to wind— especially in the lower reaches, where it is wide and deep and flows across a broad plain. Here, giant horseshoe-shape meanders develop as the river wears away the outside bank of each curve and washes up sediment on the inside.*

In the lower reaches, the river is broad and deep and flows through smooth channels of sediment, washed down from higher up

Where it meets the sea, the river may split into several branches, forming a "delta"

▲ *A river changes dramatically in character as it runs down toward the sea. High up, it is a small stream, tumbling over rocks because it is too small to wash them out of the way. Near the sea it flows through a smooth channel of silt and mud washed down by the river from higher up, over tens of thousands of years.*

FACTS: About waterfalls

- **Where falls form**
  Waterfalls typically form where a river flows over a band of hard rock, as the water wears away the soft rock below.

- **"The smoke that thunders"**
  So much water flows over Victoria Falls in Zimbabwe—33,000 cubic feet every second— that the roar can be heard 25 miles away.

▼ *The Angel Falls in Venezuela—named after an American pilot, Jimmy Angel—is the highest waterfall in the world, plunging 3,211 feet.*

DATA: The longest rivers

- The Nile in Africa is 4,137 miles long.
- The Amazon in S. America is 4,073 miles long.
- The Yangtze in Asia is 3,891 miles long.
- The Mississippi-Missouri is 3,732 miles long.
- The Danube in Europe is 1,771 miles long.

Oceans

ALMOST THREE-QUARTERS of the world is under water. There are five great oceans: the Pacific, the Atlantic, and Indian–which all merge into the Southern Ocean around Antarctica–and the smaller Arctic Ocean. Then there are many smaller stretches of water called seas, including the Mediterranean, the Baltic, and the Red seas. Yet until quite recently, the bottom of the oceans were as mysterious and unknown as the surface of Mars. Modern ocean surveys have now begun to reveal that the landscape of the ocean bed is as varied as that of the continents, with high mountains, vast plains, and deep valleys.

FACTS: About coasts

- **Eroded coasts**
  In some places, especially on headlands, coasts are worn away by waves crashing on bare rock. Hills are cut back to sheer cliffs, leaving behind platforms of rock washed over by the waves and, occasionally, isolated stacks of rock.

- **Sandy coasts**
  In other places, especially bays, material worn away is deposited as sandy and pebbly beaches and bars across river mouths.

- **Tides**
  In most places, the sea rises then falls back again twice daily. These "tides" are created by the pull of the Moon's gravity, which creates a tidal bulge of raised water on opposite sides of the world. As the Earth turns beneath the Moon during the day, so the tidal bulge moves around the world.

▼ *Constant battering by waves and salty water gives coastlines their own unique range of landforms, including cliffs, headlands, and sandy bays.*

Beach

Crustose lichen

Sand bar

Estuary

Stack

Groyne to stop sand being washed along the beach

Headland

FACTS: About the ocean bed

- **Ocean floor revealed**
  In the last 30 years, surveys using sound equipment and robot submarines have allowed oceanographers to lift away the ocean waters to create detailed maps of the ocean floor (right).

- **Shallow margin**
  Around the edge of each ocean is a shelf of shallow water called the continental shelf. At the edge of this shelf, the ocean floor plunges to the deep ocean floor or "abyssal plain."

- **Seamounts**
  The abyssal plain is not completely flat but dotted, especially in the Pacific, with huge mountains known as seamounts, often thousands of feet high. In places, there are flat-topped seamounts, called guyots, which may once have projected above the surface and been worn flat there.

In this map of the ocean floor, the light blue is the continental shelf, the dark blue is the abyssal plain.

Sonar systems map the ocean floor by sending out high-frequency pulses of sound. The time it takes for the sound pulse to echo back from the ocean floor indicates how deep the ocean is.

 DATA: The oceans

- **SEA AREA**
  The seas cover more than 139 million square miles of the Earth's surface. The biggest ocean is the Pacific, over 63 million square miles, more than one-third of the Earth's surface.

- **WATER VOLUME**
  There is 322 million cubic miles of water in the oceans.

- **DEEPEST WATER**
  The deepest point on the Earth's surface is the Challenger Deep in the Marianas trench in the west Pacific, which is 35,818 feet deep.

Key facts: Planet Earth

Highest waterfalls

Mardalsfossen (S)(Norway)	2,425ft
Tugela Falls (S. Africa)	2,011ft
Cuquenan Falls (Venez.)	2,001ft
Sutherland Falls (NZ)	1,903ft
Ribbon Falls (USA)	1,611ft
Great Falls (Guyana)	1,601ft
Mardalsfossen (N)	1,535ft
Della Falls (Canada)	1,444ft
Gavarnie Falls (France)	1,385ft
Skjeggedal Falls (N'way)	1,378ft
Glass Falls (Brazil)	1,325ft
Krimml Falls (Austria)	1,312ft
Trummelbach Falls (Switz)	1,312ft
Takakkaw Falls (Canada)	1,200ft
Silver Strand Falls (USA)	1171ft
Wallaman Falls (Aus)	1138ft
Wollomombi Falls (Australia)	1099ft

Angel Falls (Venezuela)	3,212ft
Yosemite Falls (USA)	2,425ft

Cities

The world's biggest cities

São Paulo	18,628,000
Mexico City	18,268,000
Calcutta	13,217,000
Delhi	12,791,000
Tokyo	12,310,000
Jakarta	12,300,000
Bombay	11,914,000
Rio de Janeiro	11,227,000
Cairo	10,834,000
Dhaka	10,403,000
Seoul	10,281,000
Istanbul	10,243,000
Moscow	10,101,000
Shanghai	10,031,000
Paris	9,644,000
Karachi	9,269,000
New York	8,086,000
London	7,172,000

Continents

Asia
Area	17,135,370 sq. mile
Population	3,868,000,000
Population density (People per sq. mile)	203

Africa
Area	11,703,915 sq. mile
Population	874,000,000
Population density	65

Antarctica
Area	5,400,000 sq. mile

North America
Area	9,348,000 sq. mile
Population	470,000,000
Population density	32

South America
Area	6,885,9000 sq. mile
Population	350,000,000
Population density	49

Europe
Area	4,051,000 sq. mile
Population	729,000,000
Population density	175

Oceania
Area	3,285,730 sq.mile
Population	32,359,000
Population density	6

Population

The most populous countries

China	1,299,000,000
India	1,081,000,000
USA	293,850,000
Indonesia	222,611,000
Brazil	180,542,000
Pakistan	151,600,000
Russia	144,315,000
Bangladesh	135,255,000
Nigeria	128,254,000
Japan	127,757,000
Mexico	105,447,000
Philippines	82,670,000
Germany	82,561,000
Vietnam	81,839,000

Biggest lakes

Caspian Sea	143,229 sq. miles	Lake Ontario	7,335 sq. miles
Lake Superior	32,523 sq. miles	Lake Balkhash	7,114 sq. miles
Lake Victoria	26,817 sq. miles	Lake Ladoga	6,834 sq. miles
Aral Sea	24,902 sq. miles	Lake Chad	6,299 sq. miles
Lake Huron	24,359 sq. miles	Lake Maracaibo	5,119 sq. miles
Lake Michigan	22,298 sq. miles	Patos	3,919 sq. miles
Lake Tanganyika	12,649 sq. miles	Lake Onega	3,709 sq. miles
Lake Baikal	12,159 sq. miles	Lake Eyre	3,597 sq. miles
Great Bear Lake	12,094 sq. miles	Lake Titicaca	3,200 sq. miles
Lake Nyasa	11,149 sq. miles	Lake Nicaragua	3,100 sq. miles
Great Slave Lake	11,029 sq. miles	Lake Mai-Ndombe	3,100 sq.miles
Lake Erie	9,965 sq. miles	Lake Athabasca	2,063 sq. miles
Lake Winnipeg	9,415 sq. miles		

Richest and poorest

The world's richest countries
GNP per head in the 90s

	$US
Luxembourg	42,930
Switzerland	38,380
San Marino	34,330
Bermuda	34,950
Norway	33,470
Denmark	32,050
Japan	32,030
USA	31,910
Iceland	29,540
Finland	27,730
Sweden	26,750
Germany	26,620
Netherlands	25,140
France	24,170

The world's poorest countries
GNP per head in the 90s

	$US
Ethiopia	100
Congo, Dem. Rep	110
Somalia	110
Burundi	120
Sierra Leone	130
Guinea-Bissau	160
Malawi	180
Niger	190
Eritrea	200
Chad	210
Mozambique	220
Nepal	220
Mali	240
Rwanda	250

Mountains

The world's highest mountains

Asia

Everest	29,029ft.
K2	28,251ft.
Kanchenjunga	28,209ft.

South America

Aconcagua	22,834ft.
Ojos del Salado	22,664ft.
Bonete	22,546ft.

North America

McKinley	20,320ft.
Logan	19,524ft.
Citlaltépetl	18,406ft.

Africa

Kilimanjaro	19,341ft.
Kenya	17,060ft.
Margherita Peak	16,762ft.

Europe

Elbrus	18,510ft.
Dykh Tau	17,070ft.
Shkara	17,064ft.

Oceania

Wilhelm	14,793ft.
Cook	12,316ft.
Tasman	11,473ft.

Key facts: Planet Earth

Major rivers of the world

Nile	4,147 miles	Amur-Shilka	2,744 miles
Amazon	4,083 miles	Lena	2,734 miles
Yangtze	3,900 miles	Congo	2,718 miles
Mississippi-Missouri-		Mackenzie-Peace-	
Red Rock	3,740 miles	Finlay	2,635 miles
Ob-Irtysh	3,362 miles	Mekong	2,597 miles
Yenesei-Angara	3,100 miles	Missouri-Red Rock	2,563 miles
Yellow	2,877 miles	Niger	2,548 miles
		Plate-Parana	2,450 miles
		Mississippi	2,348 miles
		Murray-Darling	2,331 miles
		Missouri	2,315 miles
		Volga	2,194 miles
		Madeira	2,014 miles
		Purus	1,995 miles
		São Fransisco	1,989 miles
		Yukon	1,979 miles

St. Lawrence	1,900 miles
Rio Grande	1,883 miles
Tunguska, Lower	1,861 miles
Indus	1,800 miles
Danube	1,775 miles
Salween	1,770 miles
Brahmaputra	1,700 miles
Euphrates	1,700 miles
Para-Tocantins	1,677 miles
Zambezi	1,600 miles
Nelson-	
S.Saskatchewan-Bow	1,600 miles
Paraguay	1,584 miles
Amu Darya	1,579 miles
Kolyma	1,562 miles
Ganges	1,549 miles
Ural	1,508 miles

Islands

The world's biggest islands

	sq. miles
Greenland	840,000
New Guinea	305,000
Borneo	290,000
Madagascar	226,657
Baffin (Canada)	195,927
Sumatra (Indonesia)	164,000
Honshu, Japan	87,805
Great Britain	84,200
Victoria, (Canada)	83,896
Ellesmere (Canada)	75,767
Sulawesi (Indo)	73,056
South Island (NZ)	58,384
Java (Indo)	48,842

Earthquake disasters

Date	Location	death toll
464 BC	Sparta, Greece	20,000
856 AD	Corinth, Greece	45,000
856	Damghan, Iran	200,000
893	Ardabil, Iran	150,000
1038	Chihli, China	100,000
1138	Aleppo, Syria	230,000
1293	Kamekura, Japan	30,000
1556	Shansi, China	800,000
1667	Shemaka, the Caucasus	80,000
1731	Peking, China	100,000
1737	Calcutta, India	300,000
1755	Lisbon, Portugal	100,000

Date	Location	death toll
1906	San Francisco, US	3,000
1908	Messina, Italy	160,000
1920	Kanshu, China	200,000
1923	Kwanto, Japan	144,000
1960	Southern Chile	5,700
1964	Anchorage, Alaska	131
1970	Ancash, Peru	66,000
1976	Tangshan, China	655,000
1985	Michoacán, Mexico	9,500
1994	Northridge, US	60
1995	Kobe, Japan	5,200

Sea deeps

The deepest sea trenches

	feet from sea level
Mariana	35,826
Tonga	35,433
Philippine	32,995
Kermadec	32,963
Izu-Ogasawara	32,087
Kuril	31,332
North New Hebrides	30,102
New Britain	29,331
Puerto Rico	28,232
Yap	27,976

Weather

The world's sunniest place is the Eastern Sahara, with sunshine for over 90% of all daylight hours.

The world's hottest place is Dallol, Ethiopia, with an average temperature of 93°F in the shade.

The world's driest place is the Atacama Desert in Chile, with an annual average of just ⅕ inch of rain.

The world's coldest place is Vostok in Antarctica, where it averages -72.°F.

Glaciers

The world's longest glaciers

Lambert-Fisher Ice Passage (Antarctica)	320 miles
Petermanns Glacier (Greenland)	124 miles
Hubbard Glacier (N.America)	98 miles
Siachen Glacier (Karakoram, Asia)	47 miles
Skeidarajokull (Iceland)	30 miles
Tasman (New Zealand)	18 miles
Aletsch Gletscher (European Alps)	15 miles

Oceans & seas

Oceans

Pacific	62,644 sq. miles
Atlantic	31,830 sq. miles
Indian	28,355 sq. miles
Arctic	5,440 sq. miles

Seas

South China	1,331 sq. miles
Caribbean	1,711 sq. miles
Mediterranean	967 sq. miles
Gulf of Mexico	596 sq. miles
Sea of Japan	389 sq. miles
East China	290 sq. miles
North	222 sq. miles
Black	178 sq. miles
Baltic	163 sq. miles

The world's major deserts

	square miles
Sahara	3,500,000
Arabian	899,614
Gobi	500,000
Patagonian	259,846
Rub al-Khali	250,000
Kalahari	225,019
Chihuahuan	173,745
Taklimakan	140,000
Kara Kum	135,135
Great Sandy	130,695
Great Victoria	130,694
Gibson	120,000
Thar	100,000
Atacama	70,000
Sonoran	70,000
Simpson	40,000
An Nafud	40,000
Mojave	15,019
Death Valley	3,012
Namib	498

Quiz: Planet Earth

1. What were the first living things on Earth?

2. Exactly how many hours, minutes, and seconds does it take the Earth to spin round once?

3. In which geological period did the first humans appear?

4. There were creatures on land long before there were any in the sea: true or false?

5. Coal is the fossilized remains of swamp plants: true or false?

6. How thick is the Earth's mantle–185 miles or nearly 2,000 miles?

7. What is the name of the highest mountain in North America?

8. Mt. Everest is gaining height: true or false?

9. Which continent has no mountains over 16,400 feet high?

10. Which country in South America has the wettest place on Earth?

11. Which volcano erupted and buried the Ancient Roman town of Pompeii in Italy?

12. Vulcanologists try to predict eruptions by looking for a slight swelling in a volcano: true or false?

13. The severity of earthquakes is measured on the Richard scale: true or false?

14. What is the name of the fault that sets off earthquakes in California?

15. San Francisco burned to the ground in 1906: true or false?

16. What is the name of the world's longest river?

17. Where is the longest glacier in the world?

18. Which is the biggest desert in the world?

19. Tides are created by the pull of the Moon's gravity: true or false?

20. The "abyssal plain" is the name given to which part of the ocean–the shallow edge or the deep ocean floor?

Answers:

1. Bacteria
2. 23 hours, 56 minutes, and 4.09 seconds
3. The Quaternary period
4. False
5. True
6. Nearly 2,000 miles
7. Mt. McKinley
8. True
9. Australasia
10. Colombia
11. Vesuvius
12. True
13. False-it's the Richter scale
14. The San Andreas fault
15. True
16. The River Nile
17. Antarctica
18. The Sahara
19. True
20. The deep ocean floor

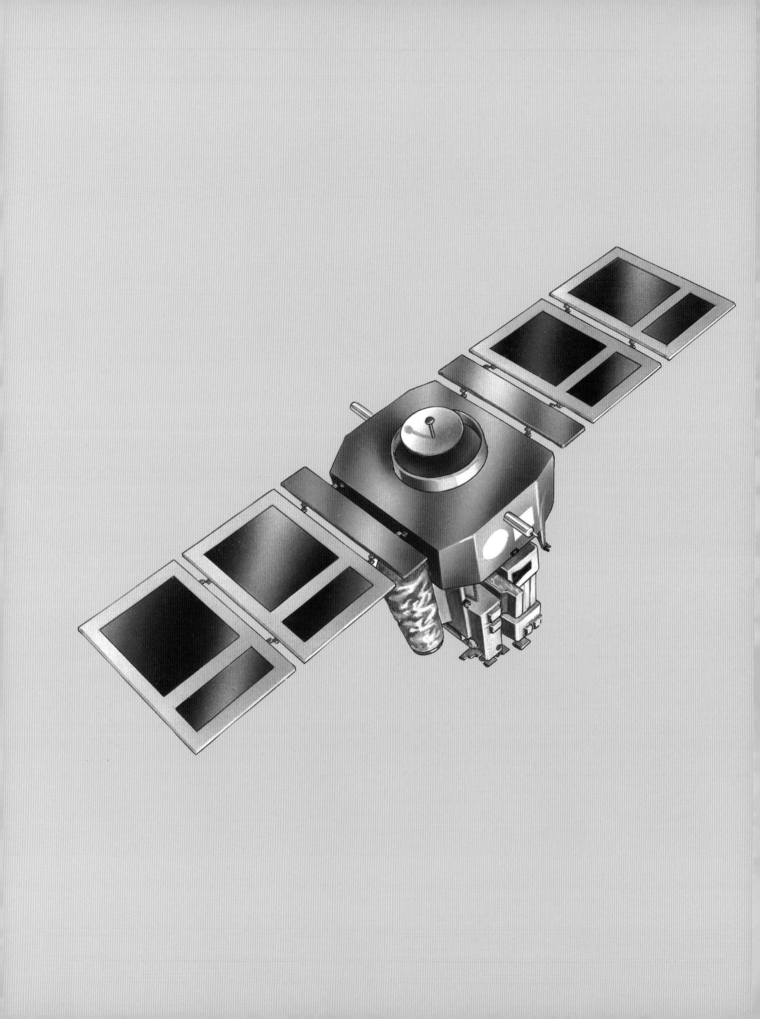

SCIENCE

Electricity

ELECTRICITY IS THE ENERGY that makes everything from toasters to subway trains work. It is also linked with magnetism. Together they form one of the basic forces that holds the universe together–electromagnetism. Electricity starts with atoms and tiny parts of each atom called electrons. Just as magnets are drawn together, so electrons are drawn to the center of the atom. This attraction is called "electric charge." Electrons have a "negative" charge; atomic centers a "positive" one. It is the combined attraction of billions of tiny electrons to billions of tiny atom centers that creates electricity.

▶ Electricity is generated in power stations and sent across the country along big cables carried on towers called pylons, or along cables buried underground. The electricity is sent down these cables at very high voltage (high pressure) to make sure they reach their destination.

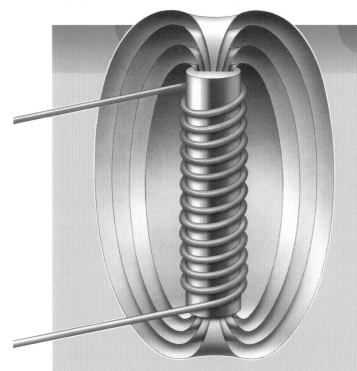

▲ If a coil of wire is wrapped around a bar of iron, switching on the current turns the bar into a very powerful magnet, called an electromagnet, or solenoid. The gray curves show lines of magnetic force.

FACTS: Electromagnetism

- **Making electricity**
  When a coil of electric wire is moved near a magnet—or a magnet is moved near a coil—the magnetism draws electrons through the wire, creating an electric current.

- **Power stations and generators**
  Power stations make electricity using generators. In generators, turbines (like fan blades) are turned by running water or by steam heated by burning oil or coal, or by nuclear energy. The turning of the turbines turns banks of electric coils around magnets.

- **Electric motors**
  Just as moving magnets create electricity, so an electric current can make a magnet move. In electric motors, an electric current is sent through a coil wrapped around a magnet. The surge of electricity through the coil makes the magnet turn.

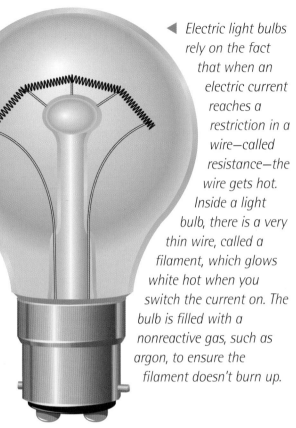

◀ Electric light bulbs rely on the fact that when an electric current reaches a restriction in a wire—called resistance—the wire gets hot. Inside a light bulb, there is a very thin wire, called a filament, which glows white hot when you switch the current on. The bulb is filled with a nonreactive gas, such as argon, to ensure the filament doesn't burn up.

FACTS: Static electricity

▶ Lightning is the release of the huge charge of static electricity made as raindrops bash together in a thundercloud.

• **Static charge**
Static electricity is what makes dry hair go frizzy when you comb it and a nylon sweater tingle if you pull it off too fast. It is called static because it doesn't move, like electricity in a circuit. It is made when surfaces rub together. Electrons rub off one surface and on to the other. The extra electrons give it a negative electric charge. This attracts surfaces, which have lost electrons and so are positively charged.

FACTS: About electric currents

• **Currents and circuits**
Electric currents can move through certain materials in a continuous flow. But for the current to flow, there must be a complete loop or circuit.

• **Free electrons**
Electric currents work like a row of marbles—flicking one jolts marbles down the row. The marbles are "free" electrons—electrons not attached to atoms.

• **Conductors**
Materials that have many free electrons, such as copper, make good conductors of electricity.

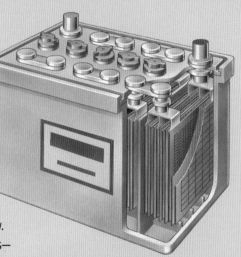

▲ Batteries use chemical reactions to create electricity. Each cell (part) has a positive and negative electrode. In a car battery, the electrodes are metal (usually lead) plates dipped in acid.

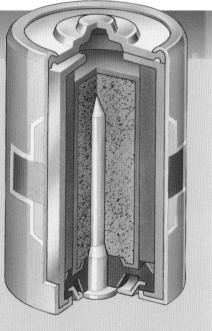

▲ Car batteries are called wet cell batteries. Flashlight batteries are "dry cells." They often have electrodes of zinc and graphite (ground carbon).

Magnetism

MAGNETISM IS THE INVISIBLE FORCE between magnetic materials, such as iron and nickel. It affects only a certain area around each magnet, called its "field." It is strongest at the two ends, or "poles," of the magnet, and gets steadily weaker farther away. Magnetism sometimes attracts magnetic materials to each other; sometimes it repels them. Magnetism works in opposite ways at each of a magnet's poles, and whether two magnets snap together or spring apart depends on which poles meet. If the same poles of each magnet meet, they push each other away. If opposite poles meet, they pull together.

FACTS: About Earth's magnetic field

• **Magnet Earth**
The Earth is a giant magnet—it behaves almost like there was a giant iron bar magnet running through its middle from pole to pole.

• **Spinning core**
The Earth gets its magnetism from its core of iron and nickel. Because the outer core is liquid and the inner core solid, they rotate at different rates. The circulating currents this createsq turns it into a giant solenoid.

• **Magnetosphere**
Earth's magnetism not only affects magnets on the surface, but also electrically charged particles 37,000 miles out in space. The vast region of space affected is called the "magnetosphere."
Without its protection, Earth would be exposed to the "solar wind," the lethal stream of charged particles whizzing from the Sun.

Lines of
magnetic force
created by
Earth's
magnetism

• **Why magnets point north**
If you hold a magnet so that it can rotate freely, it always ends up pointing the same way, with one end pointing to the Earth's North Pole and the other to the South Pole. This is how compasses work.

• **Magnetic North**
The Earth's magnetic field is slightly tilted, so compasses do not point to the Earth's true North Pole, but to a little way off northern Canada. This is called Magnetic North.

• **Magnetic dip**
Magnets not only swivel to point north but also point down. This is called magnetic dip.

▲ There is not actually a giant bar magnet inside the Earth, but it is almost as if there was. The Earth's field, constantly varies from place to place and from time to time. Scientists can work out changes that happened in the distant past from magnetic particles, frozen in rocks as they formed. This is called "paleomagnetism."

FACTS: Magnets

◄ *The effects of magnetic attraction are transmitted between objects affected by magnetism. So a magnet can pick up a string of paper clips.*

• **North and South Pole**
Every magnet has two ends: a North (north-seeking) Pole and a South (south-seeking) Pole.

• **Magnetic domains**
Cut a magnet in half and you get two little magnets, each with North and South Poles. You can go on dividing magnets into new magnets virtually down to atoms. This is because magnetic materials are made of tiny groups of atoms called domains, which are like minimagnets.

• **Curie temperature**
Iron loses its magnetic properties above 1,400°F (760°C), called the Curie temperature after Pierre Curie, the scientist who discovered this.

▼ *Lines of magnetic force may be invisible, but they are real. Around a bar magnet, they form a hamburger shape. They crowd close together around the poles, where the field is strongest.*

▲ *Auroras are spectacular curtains of light that ripple through the night sky above the poles. The northern lights, or Aurora Borealis, is seen over the North Pole and the southern lights, or Aurora Australis, over the South Pole. Auroras occur because there is a gaping hole in Earth's magnetic field over the poles, where lines of magnetic force funnel in toward them. Every now and then, charged particles from the Sun stream in through the hole and cannon into air molecules at tremendous speed. The violent collisions make all the air molecules glow so brightly they light up the sky.*

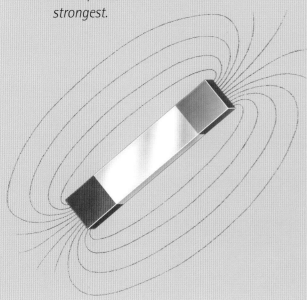

▶ *The Ancient Chinese were probably the first to make magnetic compasses, for telling fortunes as well as finding directions. But sailors everywhere have been using compasses to navigate for more than a thousand years.*

Electronics

ELECTRONICS ARE AT THE HEART of a huge range of modern technologies, from stereos to rocket control systems. All work by using electricity to send signals. Inside every electronic device there are alot of small electric circuits continually switching on and off, telling the device what to do. But electronic switches are not like electric light switches on the wall; they work automatically. The most basic switches are "transistors," which are made using special materials, called semiconductors, that change their ability to conduct electricity. Electronic systems work by linking a lot of transistors together into "integrated circuits," "chips," and "microprocessors."

FACTS: About chips and microprocessors

- **Silicon chips**
  In most integrated circuits, dozens or even thousands of tiny transistors are joined together in circuits that are packed inside a single tiny slice of silicon. This is called a silicon chip.

- **Minichips**
  Chips are getting smaller and more sophisticated by the year. This is why even complex devices such as powerful computers, can be made pocket sized.

- **Computer chips**
  The most complicated silicon chips are "microprocessors" containing a million or more transistors. These are the brains in computers.

▲ The biggest things in a silicon chip are not all its circuits and switches—the tiny patch in the center. The connectors that send its instructions to the rest of the machine—the teeth along the side of the chip—are much bigger.

▶ Televisions work by controlling a beam electronically. Inside is a "gun" that fires a nonstop stream of electrically charged particles at the screen. Where it hits, it makes the screen glow by heating up its coating of phosphor. The picture is made of thousands of these glowing spots. Electronics control just where the gun hits the screen, makes it glow, and so creates the picture.

Colors are made with three guns—one for blue, one for green, and one for red

A mask with small holes ensures each gun can only hit the right color dot on the screen

Each gun hits the right color dot–blue, red, green–and makes it glow

186

▲ *Many of the world's billions of computers are now linked down phone lines via the Internet, a system that controls all the links.*

▼ *Inside a computer are a number of microchips. At the heart is the Central Processing Unit (CPU). The CPU is what works things out, within guidelines set by the ROM, and processes and controls all the programs by sending data to the right place in the RAM.*

FACTS: About computers

- **Binary code**
  Computers work electronically. Because electronic circuits can only be on or off, computers work by using a "binary" system. This codes all data as strings of 1's or 0's—ons or offs.

- **Bits and bytes**
  Each 1 or 0 in a computer is called a "bit," and bits are grouped together into bytes. This is why a computer's memory is measured in bytes. A kilobyte is 1,000 bytes. A megabyte is 1,000,000 bytes.

- **RAM and ROM**
  Some of a computer's memory, called the ROM (read-only memory) is built into its microchips. The RAM (random-access memory) takes new data and instructions whenever needed. Data can also be stored on magnetic patterns on removable discs, or on the laser-guided bumps on a CD.

▶ *Computers are often controlled by a "mouse." Inside the mouse is a ball, which turns as the operator glides the mouse over the table. The movement of the ball moves a pointer, or "cursor," on the screen.*

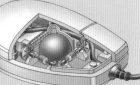

RAM   CPU (inside) where all data is processed   Slot for disk drive   Power transformer

Solar panels provide electric power for both electronic devices and motorized tasks, such as adjusting stabilizers

▶ *Satellite and space technology depends on the sophisticated and compact control provided by electronic systems. Every spacecraft has its own onboard computers, and electronic circuits allow probes to be guided through elaborate tasks over millions of miles of space.*

Radiation

RADIATION IS BASICALLY energy shot out by atoms at very high speeds. Some kinds of radiation are tiny particles splitting off from the atom. This is called radioactivity. But most radiation is tiny bursts of vibration or "waves," such as X-rays, microwaves, radio waves, and light. Light is the only form of radiation you can see; all the rest are invisible. Radiation that comes in waves is called electromagnetic radiation because it is linked to electricity and magnetism. But the length of the waves varies. The waves in gamma rays are very short, but they pack in a lot of energy, which is why they can be dangerous. Radio waves are very long and low in energy, which is why they are used for radio broadcasts. The rest come in between.

FACTS: About radioactivity and nuclear energy

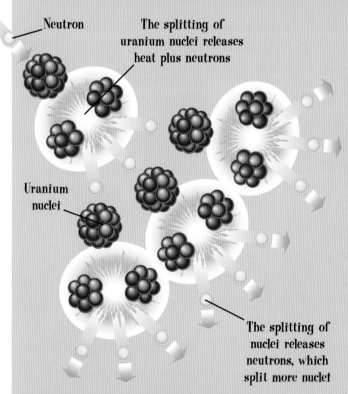

Neutron

The splitting of uranium nuclei releases heat plus neutrons

Uranium nuclei

The splitting of nuclei releases neutrons, which split more nuclei

▲ Nuclear fission relies on a chain reaction between atomic nuclei. Tiny alpha particles, called neutrons, are fired at uranium nuclei, splitting them. This not only creates heat but sets free more neutrons, which shoot away and split up more uranium nuclei, releasing more neutrons, which split more uranium nuclei and so on. Control rods in the power plant absorb neutrons and prevent the chain reaction getting out of hand.

- **Radioactivity.**
  Radioactivity is when an atom breaks down or "decays," sending out radiation: lethal gamma rays (invisible electromagnetic waves) and two kinds of particle: "alpha" particles and "beta" particles.

- **Nuclear radiation**
  Nuclear bombs and energy both create radioactive material. Radioactivity from bombs is huge, controlled and dangerous, causing death and radiation sickness and deforming unborn babies.

- **Nuclear fission and fusion**
  In nuclear power stations, huge amounts of energy are released as heat from the nuclei of atoms by splitting them. This is called nuclear fission. Inside stars and in nuclear bombs, on the other hand, vast amounts of energy are unleashed when atomic nuclei are pushed together. This is called nuclear fusion.

▶ Nuclear bombs are the most devastatingly powerful bombs of all. They release so much energy so quickly that anything nearby is turned to dust, which billows up in a huge mushroom-shape cloud.

FACTS: Scans and X-rays

▼ CT scans create a 3D picture of the inside of the body by making a complete circuit of the body along a particular "slice" with X-rays. A computer then constructs the X-ray slices into a 3D picture.

The waves are scattered around the oven by a fan

Microwaves are created by a device called a magnetron

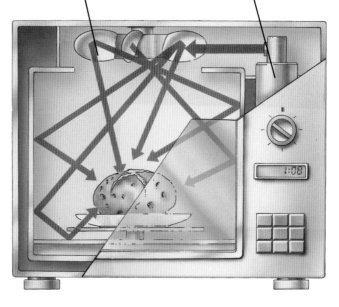

The patient is fed through the scanner as the X-ray gun rotates around her

▲ Microwave ovens work by bombarding food with invisible microwaves. It is because they are electromagnetic that microwaves heat food so quickly. Molecules of water in the food are like magnets and they are turned to and fro so quickly by the electromagnetic vibrations that they get very hot very quickly.

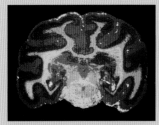

◀ SQUID scans pick up the tiny radiation from firing nerve cells, and so show the brain working in detail.

- X-rays
  X-rays can be picked up on photos just like light, even though we can't see them. They have enough energy to pass clean through skin but are stopped by muscle and bone. So muscle and bone show up in silhouette on an X-ray photo, giving doctors a vital view inside the body to help reveal problems.

- PET scans
  PET (Positron Emission Tomography) scans detect particles called positrons to show blood moving.

DATA: Radiation

- SPEED
  All electromagnetic radiation moves at the speed of light, 186,000 miles per second.

- RADIOACTIVE MATERIALS
  Uranium is one of 50 radioactive materials that occur naturally. Plutonium is one of 2000 manufactured types.

- HALF LIFE
  Half the atoms in a bit of strontium decay radioactively in just 9 minutes. In uranium it takes 4.5 billion years.

189

Light

LIGHT IS JUST ONE OF THE FORMS of electromagnetic radiation, but it is vital to us. It is the only form we can see–and without it we could see nothing. Plants grow by soaking up light, too, and changing it into food. And light from the sun provides most of our warmth and energy. Yet although we are surrounded by light during the day, very few things give out light. The Sun, the stars, electric lights, and other things that glow are sources of light. But most things you see only because they reflect light from light sources. If they do not send out or reflect light, they are invisible, such as air.

FACTS: About reflection and refraction

- **See-through**
  When light rays hit something, they bounce off, are absorbed, or pass through. Anything that lets light through, such as glass is "transparent." If it jumbles it on the way, such as frosted glass, it is "translucent." If it stops light altogether, it is "opaque."

- **Reflection**
  When light strikes a surface,

some or all is reflected. From most surfaces it scatters in all directions. But from mirrors and shiny surfaces, it bounces off in the same pattern it arrived, giving a mirror image.

- **Refraction**
  When light goes into something transparent, such as glass or water, the rays are bent or "refracted." This happens because light travels slightly slower in glass or water.

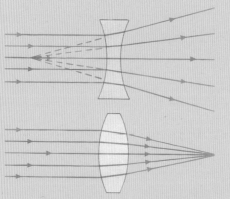

◀ The refraction (bending) of light by water makes a straw in water look as if it is bent up in the middle. Of course, it is completely straight.

▲ When light is reflected off a mirror, it is reflected at just the same angle. The angle it hits, called the "angle of incidence," is the same as the "angle of reflection."

▲ Glass lenses are shaped so that light is refracted in certain ways. Concave lenses (above) spread them out. Convex (below) lenses focus them (bring them together).

▲ Combinations of lenses in binoculars and telescopes gather light rays together to make things look bigger and closer.

FACTS: About light waves

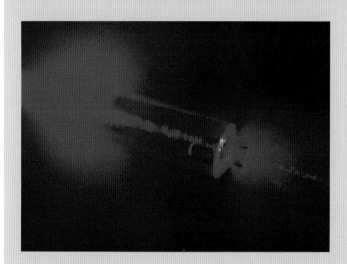

▲ *Most light contains a jumbled mixture of wavelengths. This is called "incoherent" light. But in laser light, all the waves are the same length and travel in step. This is called "coherent" light.*

- **Light waves**
  Light travels in waves, like ripples on a pond. The waves are tiny—2,000 would fit across a pinhead.

- **Light packets**
  A light beam is made up of millions of tiny packets of energy called photons.

- **Wavelength**
  Every photon has its own distinctive wavelength. The color we see depends on the wavelengths of the photons.

- **Light from atoms**
  All light comes from atoms. When an atom is energized by, say, an electric spark or by heat, it becomes "excited" and its electrons are moved. As they settle back to their normal position, they let fire a photon.

FACTS: About color

- **Color**
  When we see different colors, we are seeing different wavelengths of light. Light that contains an equal mix of all colors, like sunlight, appears white.

- **Red apples**
  The colors of objects depends on what wavelengths they soak up and what they reflect. A red apple is red because it soaks up every color but red, and only bounces red back to your eyes.

- **Primary colors**
  You can make any color of light by mixing red, green, and blue light. You can make any color of paint by mixing cyan (a bluish color), magenta (a reddish color), and yellow paint.

▲ *Different colors are refracted different amounts. So white light splits into all the colors of the rainbow when it passes through a prism (a triangular block of glass).*

Levers & machines

IN EVERYDAY LIFE, we take advantage of all kinds of machines, from toasters to TVs. But for a scientist, a machine is a device that makes life easier by reducing the effort needed to move something. There are always two forces involved in such a machine: a "load" that is the force the machine is designed to overcome; and the "effort," which is the force used to move the load. The amount a machine cuts the effort you need to move a load is called the mechanical advantage. The mechanical advantage tells you how effective any machine is, whether it is a set of gears or a lever or a crane.

FACTS: About gears

- **How gears work**
  Gears can reduce work by spreading the effort over a greater distance. This can make it easier to cycle uphill or for a car to accelerate from a standstill. They are pairs of wheels of different sizes that turn one another. They often have interlocking teeth to avoid slipping.

- **Gear ratio**
  The number of times the wheel that is driving turns the wheel that is driven is called the gear ratio. With a ratio of 5:1, the driving wheel turns five times for every time the driven wheel turns.

▶ *Inside a transmission, there are four or five pairs of gear wheels. Changing gear means selecting the right pair for the best combination of speed and force to be transmitted from the engine to the wheels.*

▼ *The pedal wheel and cogs on a bicycle wheel don't actually touch, but they are gears too—the chain connects them just like the teeth on gear wheels.*

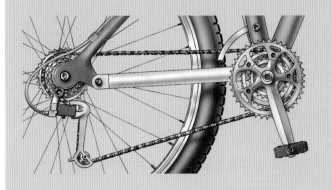

- **Increasing force**
  With a big gear ratio, the driven wheel turns slower relative to the driving wheel. But although it turns slowly, it turns with more force. This is why you select a big gear ratio to ride a bicycle uphill. Although you have to pedal much faster, pedaling is less effort.

- **Increasing speed**
  With a small gear ratio, the driven wheel turns with less force, but turns faster. This is why you select a smaller gear ratio for riding along a level road.

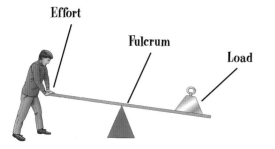

Effort

Fulcrum

Load

Some levers have the fulcrum between the load and the effort, like crowbars

Some levers have the load between the effort and the fulcrum, like wheelbarrows and screwdrivers

Some levers have the effort between the load and the fulcrum, like tweezers

▲ *A lever is a simple machine that makes it easier to move a load. If a rod is fixed at one point, but is free to swivel, it is a lever. The fixed point is called the fulcrum, and if you push on one end of the rod, your effort can be used to move a load on the other. This is called a turning effect. The farther away from the fulcrum you apply your effort, and the nearer the load is, the more your efforts will be multiplied.*

FACTS: About machines

- **Spreading the load**
  Machines do not give anything for nothing. The amount of effort to move a particular load is always the same. They make a load easier to move by spreading the effort over a greater distance.

- **Velocity ratio**
  The distance moved by the effort you apply divided by the distance moved by the load is called the velocity ratio. If the velocity ratio is greater than 1, the effort moves farther than the load. So you need less effort to move the load, but you have to apply it for longer.

- **Work**
  The sum of the efforts you put in to move something is called the "work." Work is basically the force you apply multiplied by the distance the load moves. Moving a load of 10 pounds over 10 feet always requires the same amount of work.

▼ *A mechanical digger uses powerful hydraulic (fluid-filled) systems to move its digging arms, but the same mechanical principles apply. The arms are levers and give the same mechanical advantage.*

Force & motion

A FORCE IS SIMPLY SOMETHING that pushes or pulls. Without forces, nothing in the universe would happen. Every object in the universe has its own "inertia"–that is, it will not move unless it is forced to. So if something is moving, you can be sure it has been pushed or pulled. Similarly, once it is moving, it will go on moving forever, at the same rate and in the same direction, unless some force slows it down or speeds it up or pushes or pulls it off course. This is called "momentum." It is because heavy, fast moving objects have a great deal of momentum that car crashes do so much damage.

FACTS: About gravity

• **Universal pull**
Gravity is the force of attraction that holds us all on the ground and holds the universe together. In fact, every bit of matter in the universe has its own gravitational pull and attracts every other bit of matter. The strength of the pull depends on how massive things are and how far they are apart. Massive objects nearby exert a strong gravitational pull. Light objects far away exert little pull.

▼ *When you kick a ball, at first the power of your kick overcomes air resistance and gravity and the ball climbs. But after a while, air resistance slows the ball, and gravity pulls the ball down to the ground. So it loops through the air.*

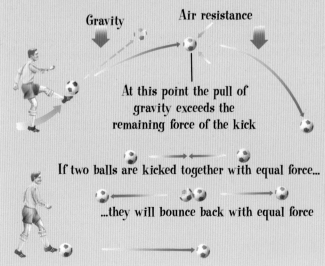

Gravity   Air resistance

At this point the pull of gravity exceeds the remaining force of the kick

If two balls are kicked together with equal force...

...they will bounce back with equal force

▶ *A tightrope walker can balance on the high wire when gravity pulls down equally on each side. This happens when the exact middle of his weight, called the "center of gravity," is directly over the wire.*

▶ *Space probes rely on gravity to pull them in toward planets. But for a safe landing, they must slow down their descent with a parachute. But this only works for small planets; the gravitational pull of massive planets such as Jupiter is too great for a parachute to have much effect.*

When you measure the weight of an apple on a spring balance—or any other way—you are simply measuring the pull of gravity. The heavier the apple is—that is, the more mass it has—the more strongly it is pulled by the Earth's gravity, and so the farther it stretches the spring on the spring balance that indicates its weight.

FACTS: Newton's Laws

▶ The great English scientist Isaac Newton (1642-1727) showed the link between force and motion in three Laws of Motion. He also discovered that the same force, gravity, made things fall and kept planets orbiting the Sun.

- **Mass and weight**
  When an object is heavy, we talk of its weight. But scientists use the word "mass." Mass is how much matter it contains. They use weight only for the force of gravity—that is, how strongly an object pulls or is pulled by gravity.

- **Acceleration by gravity**
  Like all forces, gravity makes things accelerate. Falling objects gain speed as they go down. On Earth they get faster at 32.1 feet per second.

- **Terminal velocity**
  As objects fall faster, the resistance of the air has more effect. Eventually, air resistance equals the pull of gravity and the object can fall no faster. It then falls at a steady speed. This speed is called the object's "terminal velocity."

- **Newton's First Law of Motion**
  Newton's First Law is about how an object accelerates (or decelerates) only when a force is applied.

- **Newton's Second Law of Motion**
  The Second Law is that the acceleration depends on the size of the force and the object's mass.

- **Newton's Third Law of Motion**
  The Third Law is that when a force pushes or acts one way, an equal force pushes in the opposite direction.

- **Dynamics and statics**
  The study of the way objects move when acted upon by forces is called dynamics. The study of things that do not move is called statics.

▼ Newton's laws work for everything larger than an atom that moves in the universe, from an opening bud to a speeding truck.

Energy

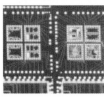

FOR ANYTHING TO HAPPEN, for things to move or even change—for chocolate to melt or a rocket to fly—you need energy. Scientists say energy is "the capacity to do work," and by this they simply mean energy makes things happen. It comes in many forms, from the chemical energy locked in sugar to the mechanical energy in a moving truck. But it always works in two ways: transfer or conversion. Energy transfer simply means it is moving from one place to another, such as heat going up a chimney or a ball being kicked. Energy conversion is when it changes from one form to another—from the steam-powered turbines to electric power in power stations, for instance.

FACTS: About solar energy

- **Solar power**
  Energy that arrives as light from the Sun gives us virtually all our energy , either directly by its warmth or indirectly by, for instance, providing the energy to grow plants which are eventually converted into coal for burning.

- **Solar panels and cells**
  Solar panels provide heat as water, sandwiched between sheets of glass, is heated by the Sun. Solar cells are light-sensitive chemicals which generate an electric current when hit by light.

▶ *Each solar cell generates only a tiny electric current, but connecting hundreds together can create a significant amount of electricity.*

▼ *Honda's record-breaking experimental solar-powered car show just what could be done with a car run entirely on sunlight.*

▼ *Less than half the Sun's energy striking the Earth reaches the ground. 53 percent of it is absorbed or reflected on the way down through the atmosphere. 16 percent of this is soaked up by water vapor and dust in the air; 7 percent is scattered by the air; 3 percent is soaked up by clouds; 23 percent is reflected off clouds; and 4 percent is reflected by the land and oceans.*

Almost one-quarter of the sunlight reaching Earth is reflected away off clouds

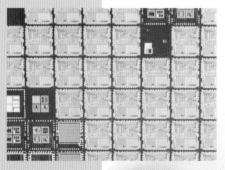

FACTS: Renewable energy

▲ *To build up water pressure to turn the turbines and to even the flow, most hydroelectric power stations are built inside big dams.*

- **Alternative energy**
  Fossil fuels are irreplaceable and pollute the air, so there is a search for clean, renewable alternatives, including electricity generated by winds, the sun (solar power), the tides, or waves.

- **Hydroelectric power (HEP)**
  HEP is electricity generated by turbines turned by water. It is the only major alternative energy source.

FACTS: Energy sources

- **Fossil fuels**
  About 90 percent of our energy comes from fossil fuels (page 161). About 40 percent comes from oil, 27 percent from coal, and 21 percent from natural gas. These sources are nonrenewable, because they took millions of years to make. So all the world's fossil fuels will eventually be used up.

- **Nuclear energy**
  Nuclear energy is also nonrenewable, but it uses fuel, such as uranium, so slowly that it will not run out in the near future. Unfortunately, it leaves a dangerous radioactive waste.

▲ *When cars burn gasoline, they not only use up a nonrenewable source of energy, they also fill the air with polluting exhaust fumes such as nitrous oxides.*

Just 47 percent of sunlight is absorbed by the ground

◀ *Flowers and other plants get their energy directly from sunlight in a process called photosynthesis. This allows them to use carbon dioxide in the air to create the energy-rich chemical sugars they need for growth. Humans, like animals, have to get their energy indirectly, by eating plants—or by eating animals that have themselves eaten plants.*

197

Heat

HEAT IS NOT JUST THE WARMTH of the Sun or a fire; it is a form of energy, the energy of molecules moving. The faster molecules move, the hotter things are. When you feel the heat of a fire, you are simply being battered by millions of fast-moving air molecules–hurried up by millions of even faster-moving molecules in the fire. The fire heats the air because heat always spreads out, and something hot always makes its surroundings warm, too, as it itself loses heat and cools down. We measure how hot something is by its temperature. But temperature is just a measure of how fast the molecules are moving; heat is the total energy of all the moving molecules.

FACTS: About conduction, radiation, and convection

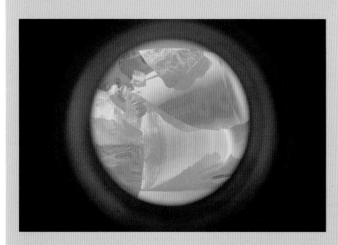

• **Convection**
Convection is when warm air rises through cool air, like a hot-air balloon. It rises because the warmth makes it expand and so it becomes less dense and lighter than the cooler air around.

◀ *Infrared radiation from the intense heat caused by silicon crystal meltdown.*

▼ *The heat of a candle flame heats up a nearby thermometer mainly by radiation, which travels in waves, just like light.*

• **Spreading heat**
Heat spreads in three ways: conduction, radiation, and convection.

• **Conduction**
Conduction is the spread of heat through substances by direct contact—a bit like a relay race, as vibrating molecules cannon into their neighbors and set them moving, too. Good conducting materials, such as metals feel cool because they carry heat away quickly.

• **Radiation**
Radiation is the spread of heat as heat rays—invisible "infrared" electromagnetic radiation (page 182). Radiation moves through space spreading heat without direct contact.

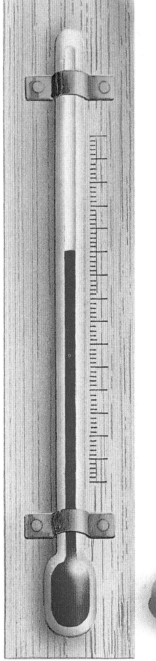

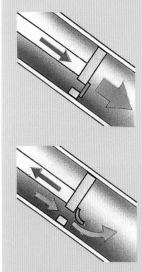

FACTS: Pressure and heat

◀ Heat makes things expand. So thermometers can measure temperature by showing how much a liquid, such as colored alcohol, expands and rises up a tube. Everyday temperatures are measured in degrees—Fahrenheit (°F) or Celsius (°C). Water freezes at 32°F which is also 0°C. Water boils at 212°F (100°C). The temperature of the surface of the Sun is 10,800°F (6,000°C). Scientists, however, would say the Sun's temperature is 6,000K, because they use a scale called the Kelvin Scale which starts at -459°F (-273°C).

◀ If air is squeezed, it gets warmer as the pressure rises. You can see this for yourself if you pump up a bicycle tire quickly. After a few pumps, it will feel quite warm. The pump works by squeezing air down through the tube with a plunger as you push down. On the upstroke, a one-way valve lets more air in.

- **What is pressure?**
  Pressure is the way water and air push against their surroundings. Molecules in air and water are always zooming about, and the pushing is actually all the molecules smashing into their surroundings.

- **Rising pressure**
  When air is squeezed, its pressure rises in proportion, because more molecules are squeezed into a smaller space. This is Boyle's Law.

- **Heat and pressure**
  If air cannot expand, heating it up boosts its pressure in proportion, because heat makes the molecules zoom about faster and smash harder into their surroundings. But if it can expand, it swells in proportion instead. This is Charles's Law.

DATA: Temperatures

- **LOWEST TEMPERATURE**
  The lowest possible temperature is Absolute Zero −459.67°F (−273.15°C), when all molecules stop moving. The lowest recorded on Earth was −128°F (−89°C).

- **HIGHEST TEMPERATURE**
  The temperature may reach 36 million°F (20 million°C) in the heart of stars. The highest on Earth was 138°F (59°C).

Solids, liquids & gases

NEARLY EVERY SUBSTANCE IN THE UNIVERSE is either a solid, a liquid, or a gas. These are said to be the three states of matter. They seem very different, but every substance can change from one to the other and back again, providing the temperature and pressure are right. Just as ice melts to water and water turns to steam when it gets hot, so every substance changes from solid to liquid to gas at certain temperatures. The temperature at which a substance melts from solid to liquid is called its melting point. The highest temperature a liquid can reach before turning to a gas is its boiling point.

FACTS: Three states of matter

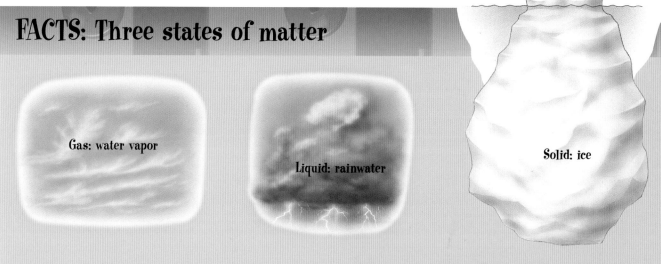

Gas: water vapor

Liquid: rainwater

Solid: ice

 ◀ A gas, like air, does not have any shape, strength, or fixed volume. This is because its molecules are moving fast enough to break the bonds that try to hold them together.

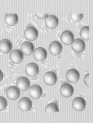 ◀ A liquid flows and takes up the shape of any container it is poured into. This is because although bonds hold the molecules together, they are loose enough to fall over each other like dry sand.

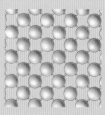 ◀ A solid has strength and a definite shape. This is because its molecules are bonded together firmly in a regular structure, and simply vibrate on the spot. The hotter it gets, the more they vibrate.

• Melting

In a solid, molecules are held together tightly by bonds and simply vibrate on the spot. Heat makes them vibrate faster, until the bonds loosen. Eventually they become so loose that the neat structure breaks down, and the substance melts and flows all over the place.

• Boiling

If the temperature goes on rising, the heat makes molecules zoom all over the place, until they move so fast that the molecules break away altogether. More and more molecules start shooting away from the surface as gas or steam. Eventually, all the liquid turns to gas.

◄ *The more firmly molecules are bonded together, the stronger and tougher solid they make. Diamond is the hardest solid of all, because all its molecules are bonded together in an incredibly strong structure.*

FACTS: About solutions

- **Special mixtures**
  Water often contains traces of other substances mixed in. If they're mixed so well that they are indistinguishable, the mixture is called a solution. Seawater is a solution of salts dissolved in water. Solutions play a vital part in our body chemistry.

- **Saturated solutions**
  When solids dissolve in a liquid, the solution becomes stronger and stronger until it becomes "saturated" and no more dissolves. If it is heated, however, more will dissolve before it becomes saturated.

Stalactite

► *Some substances turn water acid—and acids are very good at dissolving things. Rain is a mild acid and can dissolve limestone rocks—then leave the minerals it dissolves as "stalactites" in caves as it seeps through the ground.*

◄ *Sugar dissolved in tea is a solution. If you go on piling sugar in, it will eventually become saturated—the sugar molecules fill the spaces between the water molecules.*

- **Evaporation**
  As a liquid heats up, more and more of its molecules break away from the surface, turning it to gas. This is called evaporation. When clothes dry, it is because water evaporates from them.

- **Condensation**
  When a gas cools, molecules slow down until bonds form between them, forming drops of liquid. This is called condensation. Water condensing from the air is called dew.

- **Ice, water, and water vapor**
  Water is the only substance commonly found in all three states: solid ice, liquid water, and gas. Water is called water vapor when it is a gas. Steam is actually a lot of tiny drops of liquid water in air. Only when these drops evaporate does it turn to water vapor.

- **Space saving**
  Substances get smaller when they freeze as molecules pack tighter—except water. Water expands when it freezes, which is why ice bursts water pipes. It is also why ice floats, as it is less dense than water.

Stalagmite

201

Matter

MATTER IS EVERY SUBSTANCE in the universe, from the tiniest speck of dust to the largest star-everything that is not simply empty space. Surprisingly, even the most solid-looking matter is mostly empty space, too, for matter is made from tiny pieces called atoms. You cannot see them, or the space between them, because they are amazingly small. You could fit two billion atoms on the period at the end of this sentence. Scientists once thought they were the smallest things in the universe-and that they were like tiny balls that could never be split or destroyed. But they are more like clouds of energy, and they, too, are mostly empty space, dotted with even tinier "subatomic particles."

FACTS: About atoms and sub-atomic particles

• **The atomic nucleus**
The core of an atom is a cluster or "nucleus" of two kinds of particle: protons and neutrons. Protons have a positive electrical charge. Neutrons have none.

• **Electrons**
Whizzing around the nucleus as fast as the speed of light are even lighter particles called electrons. Electrons are negatively charged.

• **Atoms and ions**
Most atoms have identical numbers of protons and electrons, so the electrical charges balance. An ion is an atom that has either lost or gained electrons, so it may be either positively or negatively charged.

• **Short-lived particles**
By smashing atoms together at high speeds, scientists have found more than 200 subatomic particles besides electrons, protons, and neutrons, but most of these last only a fraction of a second.

• **Quarks and leptons**
Scientists believe that all particles are made from just two basic kinds: quarks and leptons. Electrons are leptons. Protons and neutrons are made from different "flavors" of quark.

◀ *Protons are made from clusters of three quarks, held together by gluons. There are actually six different kinds of quark but only two— "up" quarks and "down" quarks—are long-lived, and this is what protons are made of.*

▶ *Atoms are not really like this. All the particles are really just clusters of energy that probably only occur in certain places. But it is a good way to imagine them, with electrons whizzing around the nucleus.*

• **Atomic forces**
Atoms can be split, but are usually held together by three forces—the electrical attraction between negative electrons and positive protons, and the "strong" and "weak" nuclear forces that bind together the particles of the nucleus. These forces, together with gravity, are the basic forces that hold the universe together.

FACTS: About crystals

- **Crystal shapes**
  Crystals are hard, shiny solids formed in regular geometric shapes. Grains of salt, sugar, and sand are all crystals. So are diamonds. Each is made from a very regular structure of atoms, ions, or molecules.

- **Crystallization**
  When melted substances turn solid or dissolved substances leave solutions, they form crystals. This is called crystallization.

- **Crystallography**
  Crystallography is the study of crystals, usually using X-rays (page 189).

▲ *Most hard substances are crystals. A powerful microscope reveals the regular structure of crystals of sulfur. The colors are computerized.*

Water molecule

◀ *Atoms rarely exist alone. Usually they join up in small groups called molecules. Hydrogen atoms, for instance, exist in pairs or joined to other atoms. A molecule of hydrogen gas is a pair of hydrogen atoms. A water molecule is a pair of hydrogen atoms joined to an oxygen atom.*

Nucleus of protons and atoms

Around the nucleus whirl clouds of tiny negatively charged electrons

▶ *The study of matter is called chemistry. In the past, most chemistry was done in laboratories— boiling and mixing chemicals in flasks and test tubes. Now, a great deal of chemistry is done on computer, constructing molecules in cyberspace. In this way, chemists have been able to create entirely new chemicals.*

The elements

ALL THE SUBSTANCES IN THE UNIVERSE are made up from 100 or so basic chemicals, or "elements," such as gold and oxygen. Each element has its own unique character-and its own special atoms. Each element has a different number of protons and electrons in its atoms, from hydrogen with one of each to lawrencium with 103. The number of protons and electrons in their atoms is really the only difference between the elements, but this difference has a huge effect on their nature. Nitrogen gas atoms, for instance, have seven protons and carbon have six, just one less, but they are completely unlike.

FACTS: Groups and periods

- **Rows and columns**
  The Periodic Table of elements is laid out in rows called "periods" and columns called "groups."

- **Electron shells**
  Electrons spin around atoms in up to 7 layers or "shells." There is a limit to how many electrons that can fit in each shell. Only 2 fit in the first shell, closest to the nucleus, 8 in the second, and 8 in the third. After that it gets complicated, but the outer shell never holds more than 8.

- **Shells and periods**
  The number of electron shells an atom has increases down each group. So every atom in each period has the same number of electron shells. What varies is the number of electrons.

- **Electrons and groups**
  Each group is for elements with a certain number of electrons in their outer shells—and this is what determines an element's chemical properties. Every element in the same group has similar properties.

- **Reactive to stable**
  Each period starts on the left with a highly reactive "alkali metal," which has one electron in its outer shell. It ends on the right with a stable "noble gas," such as argon, which has eight electrons in its outer shell.

▼ All the elements can be displayed in order on a chart called the Periodic Table. The number of protons an element has in each of its atoms is called its Atomic Number, and the chart lists elements in Atomic Number order, starting with hydrogen at 1.

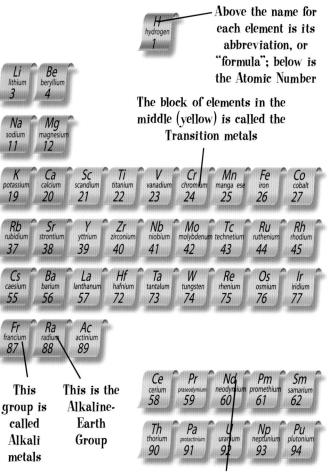

Above the name for each element is its abbreviation, or "formula"; below is the Atomic Number

The block of elements in the middle (yellow) is called the Transition metals

This group is called Alkali metals

This is the Alkaline-Earth Group

This row, called the lanthanides or rare earths, fits into Group 3

FACTS: About atomic mass and formulae

- **Atomic mass**
  Atomic mass is the "weight" of an atom of an element and corresponds to the average number of protons and neutrons in the nucleus.

- **Formula**
  Every element has a short name, or formula. Carbon is C, Hydrogen is H, Copper Cu, and so on.

▲ Atoms of gold have 79 protons in their nuclei, and, on average, 118 neutrons. So its (relative) atomic mass is 197. The formula for gold is Au.

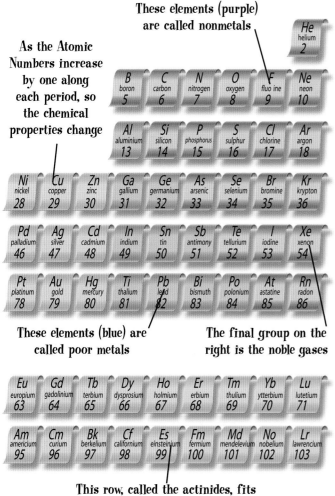

These elements (purple) are called nonmetals

As the Atomic Numbers increase by one along each period, so the chemical properties change

These elements (blue) are called poor metals

The final group on the right is the noble gases

This row, called the actinides, fits into Group 3

FACTS: About metals

- **Metals**
  Metals are hard, dense, shiny solids. They conduct heat well. They are also good conductors of electricity because they are electropositive, which means electrons easily become "free" (page 183).

- **Transition metals**
  Transition metals are metals in the middle of the table like gold—shiny and tough, but easily shaped.

- **Lanthanides or rare earths**
  These silvery metals are called rare earths because they were once thought too reactive to stay in the ground unmixed with other elements for long.

FACTS: About noble gases

- **Nobly aloof**
  Group 0 is the far right group called the noble gases. The outer shells of their atoms are full up, so they do not react with other elements. They are sometimes called inert gases.

- **Bulb gases**
  Noble gases, such as argon and krypton, are used in lightbulbs because they are unreactive.

Chemicals & compounds

SOME SUBSTANCES, such as gold, are made of just one element. Most are made of two or more elements joined together to make what is called a compound. Table salt, for instance, is a compound of the two elements sodium and chlorine. A compound is usually very different in nature from the two elements that make it up. Sodium, for instance, is a metal that fizzes and gets hot when dropped in water; chlorine is a thick, green gas.

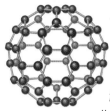

◀ One of the most remarkable molecules is this molecule built from carbon atoms called a buckyball. It was constructed by scientists as an experiment but may well have practical uses in the future.

FACTS: About chemical bonds

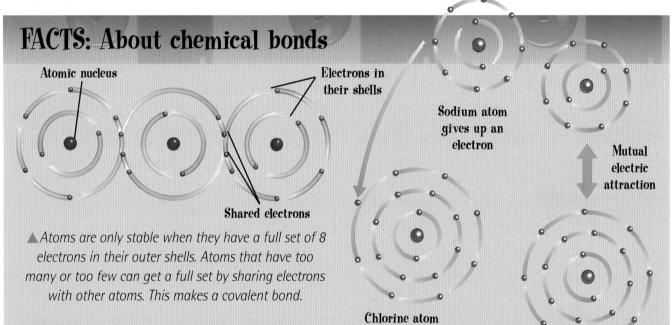

Atomic nucleus

Electrons in their shells

Shared electrons

Sodium atom gives up an electron

Mutual electric attraction

Chlorine atom gains an electron

▲ Atoms are only stable when they have a full set of 8 electrons in their outer shells. Atoms that have too many or too few can get a full set by sharing electrons with other atoms. This makes a covalent bond.

▲ In ionic bonds, one atom donates an electron to another and so becomes negatively charged. The atoms are then bonded by mutual electrical attraction. This is what joins sodium atoms to chlorine atoms in salt.

• Valency
Each atom joins only with a certain number of others—as if each only has so many hooks it can hang others on. This number is called its "valency."

• Chemical bonds
There are two main ways elements can combine: by sharing electrons in what are called "covalent bonds," or by losing or gaining them in "ionic bonds." "Metallic bonds" occur between huge numbers of atoms in a giant metallic lattice.

• Ionic bonds
Ionic bonds occur when atoms with just a few electrons in their outer shells (page 202) donate them

to atoms with just a few missing from theirs. This makes the atom losing electrons positively charged and the other negatively charged—so they stick together by electrical attraction.

• Covalent bonds
In covalent bonds, atoms share electrons. In water, two hydrogen atoms share electrons with one oxygen.

▲ Some substances make acids when they dissolve in water. Weak acids, such as lemon juice or vinegar, taste tart. Strong ones, such as sulfuric acids, are highly corrosive, burning, stinging, and even dissolving metals. The opposites of acids are bases, known as alkalis when dissolved in water. Weak bases such as baking soda, taste bitter and feel soapy. Strong ones, such as caustic soda, are as corrosive as acids. Chemists use "indicators" such as litmus paper to test for acidity. Acids turn the paper red. Alkalis turn it blue.

▼ Strong acids are dangerous, but they can be useful in many ways. Sulfuric acid is used to make everything from fertilizers to paints. Crystals of salicylic acid (below), which occur naturally in willow trees, are used to make aspirin.

FACTS: About water

▶ Water molecules are made from two hydrogen atoms and an oxygen atom arranged in a V-shape. This is why the chemical formula is H_2O.

• **Water poles**
Water molecules are special. In sharing electrons with an oxygen atom, the electrons on each hydrogen atom are tugged to the side nearest the oxygen—leaving the far side "bare," exposing the positively charged nucleus. This gives water molecules a + (positive) and a - (negative) end, and so they are called polar molecules.

• **Hydrogen bonds**
Pairs of water molecules bind together as + ends are drawn to - ends. These "hydrogen" bonds keep water liquid to 212°F, at which heat most similar substances are gases.

The sequence of chemicals that make DNA's are coded instructions

▲ The element carbon forms thousands of different compounds. Indeed, most of the "organic" compounds on which life depends are carbon compounds. The most remarkable of these is deoxyribonucleic acid, or DNA. DNA forms long molecules shaped like a twisted rope ladder. In the pattern of its rungs, DNA carries complete coded instructions for life—for everything from how a plant is to grow to what color your eyes should be.

Key facts: Science

Milestones

- 300 BC: Greek mathematician Euclid lays down the principles of geometry still used today.
- 250 BC: Archimedes lays down the basic principles of physics.
- 1665-1686: Isaac Newton introduces his theory of gravity and his three laws of motion.
- 1683: Anton van Leeuwenhoek discovers bacteria.
- 1789: Antoine Lavoisier makes the first list of chemical elements.
- 1804: Richard Trevithick builds the first steam locomotive.
- 1808: John Dalton proposes the atomic theory of matter.
- 1820: Hans Oersted finds that electricity creates a magnetic field.
- 1830: Joseph Henry and Michael Faraday find how electricity can be generated by a magnetic field.
- 1858 Charles Darwin suggests the theory of the evolution of species by natural selection.
- 1860s: Étienne Lenoir builds the first gasoline engine car.
- 1865: James Clerk Maxwell suggests the idea of electromagnetic fields.
- 1869: Dmitri Mendeléev creates the Periodic Table of the elements.
- 1897: J. J. Thomson discovers the electron.
- 1900: Max Planck invents quantum theory.
- 1903: Orville and Wilbur Wright make the first powered human aircraft flight.
- 1905: Albert Einstein invents the theory of Relativity.
- 1911: Ernest Rutherford discovers the atomic nucleus.
- 1945: The first atomic bomb.
- 1953: Francis Crick and James Watson find the structure of the DNA molecule in every living cell.

Conversions

Conversion factors
To convert, multiply by the number shown

Length
- in. to cm   2.54
- ft. to m   0.3048
- yd. to m   0.9144
- miles to km   1.6093
- cm to in.   0.3937
- m to ft.   3.2808
- m to yd.   1.0936
- km to miles   0.6214

Weight
- oz. to g   28.3495
- lb. to kg   0.4536
- tons to tonnes   0.9058
- g to oz.   0.0352
- kg to lb.   2.2046
- tonnes to tons   1.104

Volume
- in.^{3} to cm^3 (cc)   16.3871
- ft.^{3} to liters   28.3169
- yd.^{3} to m^3 0.7646
- fl. oz. to m^3 28.4131
- pints to liters   0.4507
- gallons to liters   3.606
- cm^3 to in.^{3} 0.0610
- liters to ft.^{3} 0.0353
- liters to pints   2.2187
- liters to gallons   0.2773

Fast, slow

Fast phenomena
- Light   185,871,324 miles per second
- Lightning   up to 31,248 miles per second
- Earth's orbit   66,470mph
- Speed of sound in water   4,724ft per second
- Speed of sound in air   1122ft per second at 64°F
- Skydiver   620mph
- Jet stream   up to 435mph
- Tornado   280mph
- Surface wind   230mph

Fast machines
- Fastest steam locomotive   126mph by the *Mallard* in 1934.
- Fastest train   320mph by French TGV in 1990.
- Fastest road car   217mph by Jaguar XJ220 in 1992.
- Fastest speed on land   763mph by *Thrust SSC* in 1997.
- Fastest jet plane   2242mph by Lockheed SR-71A in 1990.
- Fastest airliner   1608mph by Russian Tupolev Tu-144.
- Fastest human flight   24792mph by crew of *Apollo 10* spacecraft in 1969.

Dead slow
- Fingernails grow at around 1/50 inch a week.
- Toenails grow at about 1/250 inch a week.
- Continents move at around 16 inches a year.
- Snails move at up to 0.005mph.
- A tortoise moves at 0.17mph.
- Glaciers flow at 0.0003mph.
- Lichen grows at 0.00000000006mph.

Loud, soft

Loud noises
- Supernova explosion   210 decibels
- Rocket launch   180 db
- Toy guns   170 db
- Jet taking off at 30 m   140 db
- Rock concert   130 db
- Loud scream   128 db
- Racing car   125 db
- Dance club   117 db
- Car horn   110 db
- Chainsaw   100 db
- Thunder   90 db

Quiet sounds
- Ant breathing   less than 0 db
- The quietest we can hear   0 db
- Rustling leaves   10 db
- Quiet whisper   12 db
- Average whisper   20 db
- Conversation   40 db
- Empty theater   45 db

Key facts: Science

Number power

Large and small numbers

- Large numbers can have a huge number of digits. There are 17,000,000,000,000,000,000 water molecules in a single drop of water. So scientists often express large numbers in terms of "powers" of 10. This is the number of times you have to multiply 10 by 10 to give the number. So 100 is 10 to the power to 2, which is written 10^2. One thousand is 10 to the power 3, written 10^3, and so on.

- Tiny fractions can be written in the same way—as the number of times you have to divide 10 by 10 to give the fraction. So a hundredth is 10^{-2}. A thousandth is 10^{-3}, and so on.

Millions

- One million is 10 to the power 6 or 10^6.
- Ten million is 10 to the power 7 or 10^7.
- Seven million or 7×10^6 people live in New York.
- The Sun is 9.3×10^7 miles away.
- There are just over 31 million or 3.1×10^7 seconds in a year.

Billions

- One billion is 10 to the power 9 or 10^9.

- There are 6 billion or 6×10^9 people in the world.
- There are 100 billion or 1×10^{11} brain cells in your brain.

Trillions

- One trillion is 10 to the power 12 or 10^{12}.
- Your body contains 25 trillion or 2.5×10^{13} red blood cells .
- A swarm of 12.5 trillion or 1.25×10^{13} locusts invaded Nebraska in 1875.

Quadrillions

- One quadrillion is 10 to the power 15 or 10^{15}.
- There are about one quadrillion or 10^{15} ants in the world.
- There are about 10 million quadrillion or 10^{21} molecules in a single apple.

Add-ons

These prefixes have number meanings, e.g. *kilo*watt and *mega*byte.		mega	10^6	These prefixes mean different fractions, e.g. *milli*liter and *centi*meter.		micro	10^{-6}
		giga	10^9			nano	10^{-9}
		tera	10^{12}			pico	10^{-12}
		peta	10^{15}			femto	10^{-15}
deca	10^1	exa	10^{18}	deci	10^{-1}	atto	10^{-18}
hecto	10^2	zetta	10^{21}	centi	10^{-2}	zepto	10^{-21}
kilo	10^3	yotta	10^{24}	milli	10^{-3}	yocto	10^{-24}

Cold, hot

Cold and hot points	°F	°C	K
Coldest possible temperature (atoms stop moving)	-459.67	-273.15	0
Coldest temperature achieved in a laboratory	-459.399	-272.999	2
Helium melts	-458	-272.2	3
Outer space	-457	-270	4
Helium boils	-452	-268.9	5
Nitrogen melts	-344	-209.86	67
Coldest weather recorded on Earth	-128.6	-89.2	183.8
Water freezes	32	0	273.15
Butter melts	90	30	300
Human body temperature	98.6	37	310
Hottest weather recorded on Earth	136.4	58	331
Water boils	212	100	373.15
Surface of Venus	890	480	750
Coal fire burns	1,500	800	1,100
Iron melts	2,795	1,535	1,808
Gas flame burns	3,000	1,600	1,900
Molten lava	3,200	1,700	2,000
Carbon melts	6,422	3,550	3820
Surface of the Sun	10,000	6,000	6,000
Centre of the Earth	30,000	16,000	16,000
Lightning	54,000	30,000	30,000
Centre of a star	180 mill	100 mill	100 mill
Centre of an H-bomb	700 mill	400 mill	400 mill

Tiny, big

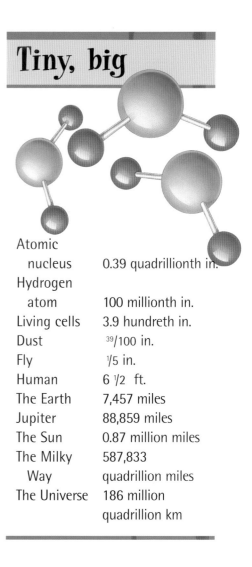

Atomic nucleus	0.39 quadrillionth in.
Hydrogen atom	100 millionth in.
Living cells	3.9 hundreth in.
Dust	39/100 in.
Fly	1/5 in.
Human	6 1/2 ft.
The Earth	7,457 miles
Jupiter	88,859 miles
The Sun	0.87 million miles
The Milky Way	587,833 quadrillion miles
The Universe	186 million quadrillion km

Light, heavy

Photon	11.7×10^{-63} lb
Oxygen atom	6.6×10^{-26} lb
Ant	2.2×10^{-5} lb
Human	2.2×10^{2} lb
Elephant	2.2×10^{4} lb
Blue whale	2.2×10^{5} lb
Oil tanker	2.2×10^{8} lb
The Earth	13.2×10^{24} lb
The Sun	4.4×10^{30} lb
The Galaxy	4.4×10^{41} lb
The Universe	2.2×10^{51} lb

Quiz: Science

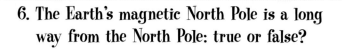

1. What is the boiling point of water?

2. Lightning is the release of a huge charge of what kind of electricity?

3. Who made the first magnetic compasses and used them for fortune telling and direction finding?

4. Iron loses its magnetism above 1,400°F: true or false?

5. Every magnet has two poles, no matter what its shape: true or false?

6. The Earth's magnetic North Pole is a long way from the North Pole: true or false?

7. What do solar cells do?

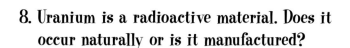

8. Uranium is a radioactive material. Does it occur naturally or is it manufactured?

9. When light rays are bent by something, such as glass or water, what is this called?

10. The angle that light strikes a mirror is called the angle of incidence: true or false?

11. What is the name of the force that holds you on the ground?

12. How many Laws of Motion did Isaac Newton find?

13. What does HEP stand for?

14. Does heat make things contract or expand?

15. Scientists think quarks are stuck together by gluons: true or false?

16. All particles are either quarks or leptons: true or false?

17. Chemists can try out new molecules on computer screens: true or false?

18. On the Kelvin scale used by scientists, water freezes at 273.15 K: true or false?

19. What is the name given to the Southern Lights (the aurora) over the South Pole?

20. What is produced when two or more elements join together?

INDEX

218

Acknowledgements

All photographs from
Miles Kelly Archive